Frank Palmer

Grammar

Second Edition

Penguin Books

PENGUIN BOOKS

Published by the Penguin Group
27 Wrights Lane, London W8 5TZ, England
Viking Penguin Inc., 40 West 23rd Street, New York, New York 10010, USA
Penguin Books Australia Ltd, Ringwood, Victoria, Australia
Penguin Books Canada Ltd, 2801 John Street, Markham, Ontario, Canada L3R 1B4
Penguin Books (NZ) Ltd, 182–190 Wairau Road, Auckland 10, New Zealand

Penguin Books Ltd, Registered Offices: Harmondsworth, Middlesex, England

First published in Pelican Books 1971
Second edition 1984
Reprinted in Penguin Books 1990
10 9 8 7 6 5 4 3 2 1

Filmset, printed and bound in Great Britain by
BPCC Hazell Books
Aylesbury, Bucks, England
Member of BPCC Ltd.
Set in VIP Times

to Stuart, John and Christopher

"*I miss the good old days when all we had to
worry about was nouns and verbs.*"

Grammar

F. R. Palmer was educated at Bristol Grammar School and
New College, Oxford. From 1950 to 1960 he was Lecturer in
Linguistics at the School of Oriental and African Studies,
University of London, where he undertook research into
Ethiopian languages. In 1952 he spent a year in Ethiopia
studying that country's languages – Tigrinya, Tigre, Bilin and
Agaw. He became Professor of Linguistics at University
College, Bangor, in 1960, and was Professor of Linguistic
Science at the University of Reading from 1965 to 1987. He has
lectured in most of the countries in Europe, in North and South
America, as well as in Africa, India, China and Indonesia. He
is a Fellow of the British Academy.

Professor Palmer was the editor of the *Journal of Linguistics*
from 1969 to 1979. His publications include *The Morphology of
the Tigre Noun*, *Semantics*, *Modality and the English Modals*
and *The English Verb*.

Contents

1 Grammar and Grammars

'The question is,' said Alice, 'whether you can make words mean different things.'

'The question is,' said Humpty Dumpty, 'which is to be master – that's all.'

Alice was much too puzzled to say anything, so after a minute Humpty Dumpty began again. 'They've a temper most of them – particularly verbs, they're the proudest – adjectives you can do anything with, but not verbs – however, I can manage the whole lot! Impenetrability! That's what I say!'

LEWIS CARROLL. *Through the Looking-Glass.*

1.1. Why study grammar?

Alice had almost certainly learnt some grammar at school. It is almost equally certain that she was bored by it. In more recent times, most school children have been spared the boredom, because the teaching of grammar has been dropped from the syllabus and, unlike Alice, they may well never know the difference between an adjective and a verb.

Yet this is an extraordinary and quite deplorable state of affairs. Few areas of our experience are closer to us or more continuously with us than our language. We spend a large part of our waking life speaking, listening, reading and writing. The central part of a language (its 'mechanics', its 'calculus' – other metaphors will do) is its grammar, and this should be of vital interest to any intelligent educated person. If it has not been of such interest, then the fault must be in the way in which it has been presented, or in the failure to recognize its importance within this essentially human activity, language.

Man is not well defined as *homo sapiens* ('man with wisdom'). For what do we mean by wisdom? More recently anthropologists have talked about 'man the tool-maker', but apes too can make primitive tools. What sets man apart from the rest of the animal kingdom is his ability to speak; he is 'man the speaking animal'

9

– *homo loquens*. But it is grammar that makes language so essentially a human characteristic. For though other creatures can make meaningful sounds, the link between sound and meaning is for them of a far more primitive kind than it is for man, and the link for man is grammar. Man is not merely *homo loquens*; he is *homo grammaticus*.

We can see this point more clearly if we look briefly at the idea of communication. Men have for centuries been interested in the language they speak, but only in recent years have they attempted to examine it in an objective or 'scientific' way. Some scholars, in their resolve to look at language without prejudice and preconception, have begun with the premise that language is a communication system and as such can and must be compared with other communication systems. Some such systems are those used by animals. The gibbons, for instance, have at least nine different calls. It has been claimed that bees have a complicated system of dances to indicate the direction, the distance and the quantity of newly discovered nectar. Other systems are mechanical; traffic lights, for instance, use three different colours, but give four different signals (in some countries five, where green as well as red combines with amber). All of these seem to have something in common with language. They all have something to communicate and they all have their own ways of communicating it.

Can we say that these communication systems have grammars – and if not, why not? The study of these other systems has not proved to be very helpful in the detailed understanding of language, though it has helped us to see the ways in which language differs from them. The main difference here is the enormous complexity of language, and it is within this complexity that we must look for grammar. A gibbon call has merely a meaning such as 'danger' or 'food', and there are only nine or so different calls. The bees can tell only the direction, the distance and the amount of the nectar. The traffic lights can only signal 'stop', 'go', etc. But the possible sentences of English with all the possible meanings are myriad or, more probably, infinite in number. We do not learn the meaning of each of all these countless sentences separately. This is shown by the fact that many, if not most, of the sentences we produce or hear are new, in the sense that they are not identical with sentences that we have produced or heard before (and some have never been produced or heard by anyone), yet we understand their meaning.

There is a highly complex system in their construction, and this complex system differs from language to language – that is why languages are different. Within this system there is a complex set of relations that link the sounds of the language (or its written symbols) with the 'meanings', the message they have to convey.

In the widest sense of the term, grammar is that complex set of relations. According to one definition, the grammar of a language 'is a device that . . . specifies the infinite set of well-formed sentences and assigns to each of them one or more structural descriptions'. That is to say it tells us just what are all the possible sentences of a language and provides a description of them. This is no small task, but one that is well worthy of human study.

It is a sad fact that we are very ignorant of some important aspects of speech. We have very little idea of the steps by which men came to speak and, indeed, no accurate assessment of the time at which speech began. At some time in the past man developed his speech organs; these were originally designed for eating and breathing, but became highly specialized for the purpose of speech. We do not know when or how this took place, for the organs are all of flesh and do not survive in fossil remains, and only a little can be conjectured from the shape of the jaw. In any case, if we knew how and when these organs developed this would tell us only how man came to master the sounds of language. It would tell us nothing about the development of the grammatical systems. The evidence for these goes back only as far as we have written records, a mere few thousand years, a tiny fraction of the total time that man has been speaking.

We are ignorant too of the neurophysiological mechanisms that make speech, and grammar in particular, possible. We know that speech is normally located in the left hemisphere of the brain, though it is a remarkable fact that if this part is damaged in early childhood speech is still developed. Since in such cases another part of the brain is used it would seem that no part of the brain is especially adapted for speech.

There are three characteristics of language that are important for the understanding of the nature of grammar: it is complex, productive and arbitrary.

That language is highly complex is shown by the fact that up to now it has not proved possible to translate mechanically from one language to another, with really satisfactory results. Some stories, as, for instance, the one of the computer that translated 'out of sight, out of mind' as 'invisible idiot', are no doubt apocryphal, but it is true that the best programmed computer still cannot consistently translate from, say, Russian into English. The fault lies not in the computer but in the failure to provide it with sufficiently accurate instructions, because we are still unable to handle this vastly complex system. It has been suggested, moreover, that from what we know about language and the human brain speech ought to be impossible. For it has been calculated that if any of the known methods of computing language were used in the neurophysiological processes of the brain, it would take several minutes to produce or to understand a single short sentence! Part of the task of the grammarian is, then, to unravel the complexities of languages, and, as far as possible, simplify them. Yet total description of a language is an impossibility at present and even in the foreseeable future.

Secondly, language is productive. We can produce myriads of sentences that we have never heard or uttered before. Many of the sentences in this book have been produced for the first time, yet they are intelligible to the reader. More strikingly, if I produce a sentence with completely new words, e.g. *Lishes rop pibs*, and ask the reader to assume that this is a real English sentence, he will be able to produce a whole set of other sentences or sentence fragments based upon it, e.g. *Pibs are ropped by lishes*, *A lish ropping pibs*, etc. It is clear that we have some kind of sentence-producing mechanism – that sentences are produced anew each time and not merely imitated. One task of grammatical theory is to explain this quite remarkable fact. As we shall see, many grammatical theories have failed in this, but one solution is considered in the final chapters.

Thirdly, language is arbitrary. There is no one-to-one relation between sound and meaning. This accounts for the fact that languages differ, and they differ most of all in their grammatical structure. But how far are these differences only superficial, in the shape of the words and their overt patterns? Some scholars would maintain that 'deep down' there are strong similarities – even 'universal' characteristics, disguised by the superficial features of sound (and perhaps of meaning). It is not at all clear how we can find the answer to this problem. When we discuss grammar, however, we assume that many characteristics of language are shared. For this reason we talk of 'nouns', of 'verbs', of 'gender' or of 'number' and other such grammatical categories. These are discussed in detail in the next section.

1.2 What is grammar?

There is a great deal of confusion about grammar because of the very many different ways in which the term is used in ordinary speech. Let us take a brief look at some of them. All of the following I would regard as misconceptions.

1. *A grammar of a language is a book written about it.* The word 'grammar' is often used to refer to the book itself – school children may often ask 'May I borrow your grammar?' It is obvious, of course, that a grammar in this sense means a grammar book, a book about grammar, but there is a real danger that even if this is accepted, it may still be thought that, even if the grammar is not the book itself, it is at least what is in the book. But in this sense the grammar of the language is no more than the grammar as presented by the author of the book.

2. *The grammar of the language is found only in the written language – spoken languages have no grammar or at least fluctuate so much that they are only partially grammatical.* This viewpoint has been supported by the etymology of the word 'grammar' – it comes from the Greek word meaning 'to write'. This is an important widespread belief, and I shall spend a whole section considering it (1.4, pp. 27–34). It is enough to comment here that in this sense languages which have never been written down would be said to have no grammar. But this we cannot accept.

3. *Some languages have grammar, others do not: Chinese, for instance, has no grammar, and English has precious little.* What is meant by this is that English has very few 'inflections' – that each word has only a few different shapes and that in Chinese all the words keep the same shape. Whereas in Latin the verb *amo*: 'I love' has over one hundred different forms, the English verb 'to love' has only four forms: *love, loves, loved* and *loving* (some verbs have five: *take, takes, took, taken, taking*), and the Chinese word for 'love' is always the same. But this is to use the term 'grammar' in a very restricted sense. It refers to MORPHOLOGY only, which deals with the forms of words, and omits altogether SYNTAX, which is concerned with the way in which words combine to form sentences. But the order of words is a matter of syntax and syntax is a part of grammar (see 2.2). A very important part of English grammar tells us that *John saw Bill* is different from *Bill saw John* and that *a steel sheet* is different from *sheet steel*; yet in the restricted sense of grammar that we are now considering, these differences would not be deemed grammatical.

4. *Grammar is something that can be good or bad, correct or incorrect. It is bad (incorrect) grammar to say 'It's me', for instance.* This again is a widespread belief and also deserves careful consideration (see 1.3). Once again, however, notice that on this interpretation it will usually be languages that are formally taught in school or through books that are said to have any grammar. For it is at school or in books that we usually find the criteria for what is good and what is bad grammar.

5. *Some people know the grammar of their language, others do not.* This is a little more subtle. It implies that a language does not have a grammar until it is made explicit and can be learnt from a grammar book or at school. But there is surely a sense in which knowing the grammar of a language means that you can speak it grammatically. An Englishman might well be said to know the grammar of French perfectly if he spoke it as grammatically as a Frenchman, but had never attended a class or read a book about French.

It is fairly obvious from all this that I want to use the word 'grammar' in the sense suggested at the end of the last sentence. It describes what people do when they speak their language; it is not something that has to be found in books, written down or learnt by heart. As investigators, of course, we want to write about the grammar of a language; but writing it down does not bring it into existence any more than writing about biology creates living cells!

Within linguistics, 'grammar' is normally used in a technical sense to distinguish it chiefly from PHONOLOGY, the study of the sounds of a language, and SEMANTICS, the study of meaning. It lies so to speak 'in the middle', between these two, and is related in a Janus-like way to both. There is some debate still about the precise status of grammar vis-à-vis the other 'levels', as we shall see particularly in the last chapter.

Among some scholars the term 'grammar' is used in a rather wider sense to include, to some degree, both phonology and semantics, with the term 'syntax' used for the central portion. But I use the term in the narrower, more traditional sense, and this book contains therefore no detailed discussion of sound systems or of meaning.

1.3 Correct and incorrect

In the previous section I mentioned the view that grammar can be good or bad, correct or incorrect. This might seem reasonable enough. Is grammar not like manners which can and should be the subject of approval or disapproval? This view is very widespread and is, of course, related to the other views that were discussed – that grammar is something that can or must be learnt from a book, and that knowing the grammar of a language means having an explicit knowledge of it. Some years ago, for instance, I lived in Wales and made an attempt to learn the Welsh language. One of my Welsh friends on hearing this commented, 'You'll learn to speak better Welsh than we do – you'll have learnt the grammar.' The implications are clear: there is a better and a worse kind of Welsh and the better kind is to be found in grammar books – it can be learnt and so 'known'.

These misconceptions are all mixed together, but the basic mistake is seeing grammar as a set of normative rules – rules that tell us how we ought to speak and write. It is important incidentally to stress the word 'normative', since, as we shall see later, one theoretical model of grammar makes extensive use of rules; these will prove, however, to be descriptive rules (rules that describe the language), not prescriptive rules (rules that prescribe the language). That is, they will be rules that state what we in fact say, not rules that state what we ought to say.

Normative grammar teaches us to say *It is I* instead of *It's me*, to avoid ending sentences with prepositions, to know the difference between *owing to* and *due to*, to use *each other* instead of *one another* when only two people are involved, and so on. The authority for these 'correct' forms lies, of course, in the grammar books. They have been drilled into generations of schoolboys, and it is no coincidence that we speak of the 'grammar' schools. In France there is an even more impressive authority, the French Academy, which since 1635 has been the body with the right to decide what is and what is not permissible in the French language.

Most of these rules of grammar have no real justification, and there is therefore no serious reason for condemning the 'errors' they proscribe. What is correct and what is not correct is ultimately only a matter of what is accepted by society, for language is a matter of conventions within society. If everyone says *It's me*, then surely *It's me* is correct English. (For by what criterion can everyone within a society be guilty of bad grammar?) But we must be a little careful here. It is not simply a matter that whatever is said is thereby correct; I am not arguing that 'anything goes'. It depends on who says it and when. In other words, there are manners even in language. Certain language forms are regarded as uneducated or vulgar; this is a judgement that our society makes. Some forms of language are acceptable in certain situations only. At an interview for a job, for instance, we have to watch our language as well as our clothes. To use certain types of language there would be as detrimental as wearing old clothes. But most of the rules of the traditional grammar that has been taught over the years are not rules of behaviour of this kind. They prescribe forms that many of us would never normally use, and, if we do, we feel we are 'speaking like a book'. The best way of seeing that these rules have no validity is to look at the justification, or supposed justification, that is given for them.

First of all, many of the rules are essentially rules taken from Latin. Latin was the classical language known by all educated people and was once regarded as the model for all other languages. Even today there are people who say that Latin is more 'logical' than English. In the debate some years ago about the teaching of Latin at school and the requirement of Latin for entrance to Oxford and Cambridge, the familiar arguments were put forward – Latin helped to discipline the mind, Latin taught the students grammar. This latter statement was true in a rather paradoxical way. Since most English grammar teaching was based upon Latin, the students were often at a loss. They could not see why English had a subjunctive or a dative case, but when they learnt Latin it all became clear. Latin helped them with their English grammar, but only because English grammar was really Latin grammar all the time!

The rule that we should say *It is I* is a typical example of a Latin rule taken over for English. The argument (which I do not accept) runs as follows. In Latin the nouns have six different cases as exemplified by:

nominative	*mensa*	*amicus*
vocative	*mensa*	*amice*
accusative	*mensam*	*amicum*

genitive	*mensae*	*amici*
dative	*mensae*	*amico*
ablative	*mensa*	*amico*
	('table')	('friend')[1]

With the verb 'to be' the rule is that the complement must be in the same case as the subject. If, therefore, we translate *Caesar* (subject) *is my friend* (complement), the word for *Caesar* is in the nominative (subjects of finite verbs are always in the nominative) and so are the words for *my friend*. Thus we have *Caesar est amicus meus*. The same is true of pronouns, so that we find in one of the plays of Plautus, *Ego sum tu, tu es ego*, literally *I am thou, thou art I*. On the analogy of Latin, English *I* is said to be nominative and *me* accusative. Since in *It is . . . It* is also nominative as it is the subject of the sentence, it follows that we can say only *It is I* and that *It is me* is 'ungrammatical'.

The same kind of argument is used to prescribe the 'correct' reply to *Who's there?* In Latin the answer would again be in the nominative – the same case as the word for *Who*; in English we are, therefore, expected to say *I* not *me*. This reasoning also accounts for the rule that we should say *He is bigger than I*, not *He is bigger than me*. In Latin the noun being compared has to be in the same case as the noun with which it is compared, and, since *He* is in the nominative, so too must *I* be. (But we have to say *He hit a man bigger than me* because *a man* is the object and is in the accusative.)

There is no reason at all why English should follow the Latin rule. In the first place, English has no case endings for the noun (except possibly the genitive) and only a vestige of case with the pronoun – *I/me*, *he/him*, *she/her*, *we/us*, *they/them*. Secondly, though there is this rule in Latin, there are contrary rules in other languages. In French, forms that are literally *It's I*, . . . *bigger than I* are quite ungrammatical: we cannot say **C'est je*, or **plus grand que je*. *Je* cannot stand alone. French here uses the form *moi*. *C'est moi, plus grand que moi*. There is a story of an important conference at which it was asked if there was an Englishman present who spoke fluent French and one man raised his hand and cried 'Je!' *Moi* is not quite equivalent to English *me*, because French has an object (accusative) form *me* also, but

1. In this chapter I use a number of technical or semi-technical terms because it is unavoidable in this discussion. An account of the way in which they are used is to be found in Chapter 2.

the point is made – French does not allow the nominative form in these constructions. In Arabic, more strikingly, the verb 'to be' actually requires the accusative to follow it (like any other verb). If we had chosen Arabic as our ideal, *It's I* would have been as ungrammatical as *He hit I, and *It's me* the form prescribed! (It is a convention to mark forms that do not occur with an asterisk.)

Strangely enough, those who advocate these rules do not simply admit they take them from Latin. They produce specious arguments in their favour. For *It is I*, it is argued that, since *I* is identical with *it*, they must be in the same case. This is still seriously put forward sometimes, but it is utterly implausible. Is *myself* then in the nominative in *I washed myself*? Perhaps there is some feeling that there is a kind of identity or equality, as in arithmetic where $2 + 2 = 4$, but even so, what has this to do with the choice of case? A different argument is put forward for *He is bigger than I*. It is argued that *than* is a conjunction, not a preposition, and that this sentence is short for *He is bigger than I am*, *am* being 'understood'. But this will not work either. By the same token we could argue that we ought to say *He came after I on the grounds that *after* also is a conjunction and that this sentence is short for **He came after I did*. The arguments are identical, yet no one argues for *He came after I*. Why not? The answer is simple. In Latin there is both a preposition *post* and a conjunction *postquam* with the meaning 'after', but the word that means 'than' (*quam*) is always a conjunction and never a preposition. But why should this be true of English? Should we not rather treat *than* in the same way as *after* (either preposition or conjunction) and permit:

> *He came after me.*
> *He came after I did.*
> *He is bigger than me.*
> *He is bigger than I am.*

The trouble with rules like these is that people do not understand them and often misapply them. It has, for instance, become almost a maxim in English, 'When in doubt use *I* not *me*.' This is the reason for the very common occurrence today of *between you and I* and similar expressions, where *between you and me* would be 'grammatical'. As a linguist I make no judgement; perhaps *I* is now the form that is used after *and* – there would be nothing strange linguistically about this.

A rule of a quite different kind that has come from Latin is the rule that we must not end a sentence with a preposition. Educated English people know the rule but they do not obey it. Indeed, when people were being interviewed in the street for a radio talk that I gave, one man insisted that *A chair is something you sit on* was incorrect; when asked why, he replied 'Because a preposition is a word you can't end a sentence with'! In fact, it is true that Latin does not permit sentences with final prepositions, and it is even true that 'form' words, as they are often called, like prepositions and conjunctions, are not permitted at the end of a line of verse, even when this is not the end of a sentence. But again why should this be imposed upon English? It is easy enough to make fun of this rule. It is said that one of Winston Churchill's papers was altered by a secretary to avoid ending a sentence with a preposition and Churchill, restoring the preposition to its original place, wrote 'This is the kind of pedantry up with which I will not put', and there is the story of a little girl who finding her mother had brought up a book that she did not like, said 'What did you bring that book I didn't want to be read to out of up for?'

There is, then, no reason why the grammar of English should be based upon the grammar of Latin or upon the grammar of any other language. Similarly, we should never expect the grammar of any other language to be based upon that of English. It is the assumption that other languages will be like our own in their grammatical structures (as well as in their sound system and their semantics) that makes it so difficult for people to learn foreign languages. At a very early age we become conditioned to thinking that our own language does things in the 'right' or the 'natural' way and that there is something rather odd about the way other languages work. Even if we do not seriously believe it, we may well feel that the word *dog* is more appropriate to the four-legged pet than French *chien* or German *Hund*. In Aldous Huxley's *Crome Yellow* there is a sequence in which a character gazing at some pigs wallowing in the mud remarks 'Rightly is they called pigs.' There is a similar story of a little girl who made the exciting discovery that pigs are called pigs 'because they are such swine'.

Clearly none of this can be taken seriously, but in grammar the preconceptions are more deeply rooted. Consider, for instance, the fact that in English the subject of a sentence normally precedes the verb, and the object normally follows, that in *John hit Bill* we know that John did the hitting and Bill was the one who was hit. There is no logical or natural reason why this should be so; in a language like Latin which marks subjects and objects by different endings on the nouns the order of the words is not a critical fact in the meaning. The Latin sentence *Marcum vidit Caesar* (even if slightly unusual Latin) means 'Caesar saw Marcus' and not 'Marcus saw Caesar' (which would require the forms *Marcus* and *Caesarem*). Similarly, it is not a universal feature of languages to ask questions by changing the order of part of the sentence, as in English we have the statement *John can go* and the question *Can John go?* Some languages merely use intonation to indicate questions, but many have a word or particle that indicates them (Latin has the suffix *-ne*, Tigrinya, an Ethiopian Semitic language, has the suffix *-do*). In Welsh, however, the normal order of words in statements is to put the auxiliary verb first, then the subject and then the main verb. Thus *He is going* is *Mae ef yn mynd* (literally, I suppose, **Is he in going*). An English child who had to learn Welsh came home complaining bitterly that it was a very stupid language because 'every time they want to say something, they ask a question'! At a quite early age he had completely accepted a conventional device for English as a universal fact of all languages.

It is unfortunate, perhaps, that French forms its questions in a way similar to that of English, so that *Have you seen . . .?* is *Avez-vous vu . . .?* For French is the language that is most commonly learnt by English-speaking children, and it seems clear that the occurrence of the same device in French can only strengthen the feeling that it is wholly natural. Worse, it occurs also in German, and German is the second language most commonly taught in schools. This method of forming questions is not, then, a purely English convention, but it is only a Western European convention and the fact that it turns up in all three of these languages is a result of cultural contact over the centuries. But it is in no sense natural or universal.

Many traditional grammar books of foreign languages have taken it for granted that all languages have the same grammar, and usually it was assumed that this was identical with Latin grammar. In this spirit, it is reported, one grammarian remarked that Japanese was 'defective' in the gerund (the name for a particular type of verbal noun in Latin, also applied to some *-ing* forms in English). But is not Latin defective in those forms that are found in Japanese, but not in Latin?

There are many scholars who believe that there are universal features in the grammars of all languages (see pp. 193–4). But these features have proved either to be so abstract that it is difficult to show whether they are the same in all languages or very general – it may, for instance, be true that the noun/verb distinction is valid for all languages. But not all languages have tense, or number (singular and plural), and it is probably not even possible to hold that all languages have subjects and objects (see pp. 75–7). Even where such familiar grammatical terms are used in different languages, they may well have rather different meanings.

A second source of normative rules is 'logic' – I use quotation marks because the arguments are often not logical at all. Sometimes this logic is invoked to justify a rule based on something else, e.g. Latin. We have seen an example of this in the justification of *It is I*. In English the most notorious example of the logical argument concerns double negatives. Why can't we say *I didn't see nobody* or *I didn't go nowhere*? Because, the answer will be, one negative 'cancels out' another, so that these two sentences really mean *I saw somebody* and *I went somewhere*. But this is nonsense. Why should two negatives cancel each other out? Why should they not reinforce each other? The 'logic' of this is presumably based on the mathematical rule that two minuses make a plus. Yet double negatives were used in Anglo-Saxon and are not uncommon in Shakespeare. They are found in Spanish:

No dije nada 'I said nothing' (literally, 'Not I said nothing'),

and in Russian:

Nikto ne rabotal 'No one worked' (literally, 'Nobody not worked').

It was the same in classical Greek but not in Latin. This should be hardly surprising; if Latin had had double negatives they would have found favour, not disfavour, with English grammarians! There can, then, be no logical reason for excluding double negatives. No rules are broken by *I didn't see nobody*. It does not follow, however, that this sentence is 'good' English, if by 'good' we mean 'spoken by educated people'. Proving that there are no logical objections to double negatives does not show that they are acceptable in English. They are still (in the educated

form of English) ungrammatical, in the sense that they do not
conform to the accepted linguistic habits of the community. If,
however, we hear someone say *I didn't see nobody* the only
judgement we can rightly pass is that he is speaking a form of
English (perhaps a dialect) of which we do not approve. We
cannot rightly say that that dialect is any less logical than the
dialect we ourselves speak.

Sometimes 'logic' is based upon a misinterpretation of the
facts. Again, we have seen one example in the *He is bigger than
I* argument – that *than* is a conjunction and that this is short for
than I am. The argument collapses if we insist that *than* is a
preposition too and so requires *me*. A similar false argument is
found in the belief that there is something wrong with *Someone
has left their book behind* – though the Duchess in *Alice in
Wonderland* said 'if everybody minded their own business, the
world would go round faster than it does.' How, we are asked,
can the singular *someone* or *somebody* be referred to by the
plural *their*? It should be *Someone has left his book behind*. The
trouble is, of course, that it might be *her* book since *someone*
does not distinguish sex as *his* and *her* do. So what can we do?
Well, if we begin by rejecting the assumption that the sentence
is ungrammatical, we can say that *their* functions not only as the
plural possessive but also as a singular possessive when sex is
unknown (if sex is irrelevant, *its* is used). Similarly, we find *they*
as well as *he*, *she* and *it* used for the singular: *If anybody can
come, would they please let me know*. This is a common and
useful device; it is not illogical or ungrammatical, unless we
decide, contrary to our observations, that *they*, *them* and *their*
are always plural.

If we turn to other languages, the application of logic is even
more dangerous and may often be a result simply of a false
identification of the grammatical structure of that language with
our own. For instance, in Tigrinya it is possible to say what
appears in word-for-word translation to be:

> *To-your-house I-am that-I-come.*

But we might think that this ought to be:

> *To-your-house it-is that-I-come.*
> ('It is to your house that I come.')

Similarly, Japanese has what are called 'adversity passives' of intransitive verbs such as DIE, so that it can say what would be literally translated as:

> *He was died by his wife.
> (i.e. 'He suffered from the death of his wife.')

But it would be quite wrong to suggest that either this or the Tigrinya example is illogical and quite incorrect to call them ungrammatical. Languages differ in their 'logic' as well as their grammar.

Another striking example of different logic in different languages concerns the use of singular forms with the numerals. English says *one dog*, but *five dogs*, *forty dogs*, etc., using the plural *dogs* with all the 'plural' numerals. But Welsh does not: we find *un ci* 'one dog', *pump ci* 'five dogs', *deugain ci* 'forty dogs' (*ci* is singular – the plural form of *ci* 'dog' is *cŵn*). In Tigre, another Ethiopian Semitic language, the same is true though with an added refinement. Many nouns are not true singulars in their basic form, but collectives. An example would be *nəhəb* 'bees'. In spite of the English translation this is not a plural – the plural is *änhab*. A 'pure' singular, which is better called the 'singulative', can be formed by the addition of a suffix – *nəhbät* 'a bee'. But while 'one bee' is, not surprisingly, *hätte nəhbät*, 'two bees' is *kəl'e nəhbät* and 'three bees' *säläs nəhbät*; paradoxically the singulative form has to be chosen with all the numerals, even those meaning more than one. There are many other languages which do the same. But are these less logical than English? The argument can go either way – either that we ought to use a plural form of the noun because the numeral shows that we have plural objects, or alternatively that we need not use the plural form because the numeral has already marked plurality and there is no point in marking it twice. It is English that is less economical here. It has what is usually called 'redundancy', marking what is already marked. (Another quite different example was pointed out to me by a Spanish friend. Why do we say *He put his hand in his pocket*? Why *his* hand, why *his* pocket? Do we seriously expect he put someone else's hand in someone else's pocket?)

A third source of normative rules is the belief that what used to be required in language still ought to be required, the older form being tacitly accepted as 'better'. This is probably the only argument in favour of *whom* rather than *who* in *Whom did you see?* when almost everyone would say *Who did you see? Whom* is virtually dead, but is kept alive artificially by the grammarians. In Bernard Shaw's *The Village Wooing*, the following conversation occurs:

> If it doesn't matter who anybody marries, then it doesn't matter who I marry and it doesn't matter who you marry.
> Whom, not who.
> O, speak English: you're not on the telephone now.

The same attitude, no doubt, is found in the very widespread objection to the now increasing use of *hopefully* to mean 'it is hoped'. There is no argument; it is merely stated, quite dogmatically, that *hopefully* means 'with hope', and that, therefore, *He is coming, hopefully* cannot mean 'He is coming, I hope', but only 'He is coming with hope'. But there is no rational basis for this argument. Why should we not allow that *hopefully* may be used (as it is being regularly used) in both senses? For *naturally* has two similar senses. We may compare (where the comma in the punctuation shows the differences):

She speaks French naturally.	'in a natural way'
She speaks French, naturally.	'it is natural'
He's coming hopefully.	'with hope'
He's coming, hopefully.	'it is hoped'

The appeal to earlier forms of the language is particularly common in the discussion of meanings. When someone says, 'It really means . . .' they probably mean 'It used to mean . . .' A very good example of this is found in the word *nice*, which some teachers still tell children really means 'precise' or 'exact' as in *a nice distinction* or *a nice point*. But this, except in these expressions, is what it *used* to mean, not what it means now. The trouble about appealing to older meanings is that there is no obvious time at which we can stop. For, if we go back a little further, we shall find that *nice* meant 'foolish' or 'simple', not far away in meaning from the Latin *nescius* 'ignorant', from which it is derived. But the Latin word comes from a negative prefix *ne-* and a root which, though it has the meaning 'to know' in Latin, originally meant 'to cut' and is related to *schism* and *shear*. So originally it should have had the meaning 'not cutting' or 'blunt' (almost the opposite of the prescribed meaning of 'precise'). So how far back do we go for an 'original' meaning? (Note once again that the teacher may well not be wrong in dissuading the child from using *nice* since it is inelegant to write 'It was a nice day so we went for a nice walk along a nice road . . .' But this is poor style, not the use of a word with the 'wrong' meaning.)

Again, normative rules are often based upon a particular, favoured form of the language. This may be the written form (we shall be discussing speech and writing in some detail later) or it may be the standard language, e.g. standard English. English that does not conform to this is 'sub-standard'. Grammatically, then, all of the following would be sub-standard:

> *They was there this morning.*
> *He ain't coming.*
> *Don't talk to I.*
> *I seed him this morning.*

Yet all of these are perfectly possible forms in some dialects of English. Why then are they 'ungrammatical'? The answer is quite simply that they are not standard English. There is no other answer to this question. The judgement, that is to say, is essentially a social one. People who speak like this do not belong to that branch of society that we recognize as educated. But it is most important to stress that in terms of linguistic efficiency these forms are no worse than those found in standard English. It is, moreover, largely a matter of historical accident whether one form rather than another has survived in this type of English. But surely, someone may object, *seed* is ungrammatical, because the past tense of *see* is *saw*? The answer is, of course, that *saw* is the past tense in standard English. But we can go no further. It is no good appealing to history since standard English too has abandoned many of its 'irregular' past tense forms in favour of forms ending in *-ed*. For instance, British English has *dived* where American also has *dove*. Standard English no less than the dialects has lost most of its inflections and there is no reason to argue that those that it has retained are somehow more valid grammatically, in any absolute sense. In many cases, moreover, we can actually invoke history on the side of the dialects rather than the standard language. Many English dialects, for instance, retain the *thou/thee* forms with the corresponding forms of the verb. Yet forms like *dost*, *bist* (*beest*), as well as all the forms of the pronoun, would normally be regarded as sub-standard. But it would be reasonable to argue that a dialect which retains these has a greater claim to respectability on grounds of linguistic history than a dialect which has lost the distinction between *thou/thee* and *you*. Similarly, the form *'em* instead of *them* is usually considered to be uneducated. In actual fact, it is not uncommon in the colloquial speech of perfectly well-educated people. There is no historical–linguistic reason to prefer *them*; on the contrary, the *'em* form is older – *them* is a comparatively recent intruder. It is, moreover, misleading to write *'em* with an apostrophe since it is not derived historically from *them* with the loss of its initial consonant; the [ð] (*th*) was never there.

It is wrong, then, to consider the dialect form as a corrupt form of the standard. Indeed, it is always wrong to consider dialects as corrupt forms. They are not corrupt, but different, forms of the language. It may well be that they are not acceptable for many purposes, in the speech of educated people, in the mass media, etc., but this is wholly a matter of social convention, not of linguistic inferiority. This is in no way to deny the importance of social conventions. We break the conventions at our peril, we are dubbed 'ignorant', we fail to get the job we hoped for; but we ought not to provide pseudo-linguistic grounds to justify the conventions.

Finally in this section, it may be of interest to trace the origin of the normative rules. Most of them were invented by eighteenth-century grammarians and reinforced by their nine-teenth- and even twentieth-century successors. One of the most notorious was Bishop Robert Lowth who in 1762 published *A Short Introduction to English Grammar*. He was in no doubt that the aim of his grammar was to show off 'every phrase and form of construction, whether it is right or not and . . . besides showing what is right . . . pointing out what is wrong'. Many of our normative rules are to be found in Lowth, though there is one at least that was not followed up – he advocated *sitten* instead of *sat*! The most famous, perhaps, of all grammars that followed Lowth is the *English Grammar* of 1795 by Lindlay Murray, in which grammar is defined as 'the Art of rightly expressing our thoughts by words'. Strangely enough it is with Murray and his contemporaries that we find English grammar no longer being described in terms of all the grammatical categories of Latin, a practice to be found in earlier grammars such as William Lily's *Short Introduction of Grammar* in the sixteenth century. But if the Latin categories were abandoned, the appeal to Latin for correctness was not. The rule concerning prepositions at the end of the sentence was taken up with fervour by the poet Dryden, who proceeded to 'correct' all his earlier works which contained this 'error'. Normative grammar is of course still with us, but the most notorious example within the last century is J. C. Nesfield's *Manual of English Grammar and Composition*, first published in 1898 and reprinted almost yearly after that and sold in huge quantities at home and abroad. Nesfield makes no major statements about the normative aims of grammar, but two of his sections are entitled *Purity of diction* and *Propriety of diction* and normative rules abound.

1.4 Speech and writing

We mentioned earlier the misconception, supported by the fact that the term 'grammar' comes from the Greek word meaning 'to write', that grammar is concerned with the written language. The Greek for 'grammar' is *grammatikē* or *grammatikē technē*, 'the art of writing'. This connotation remains in the term 'grammar school'. From a descriptive point of view, however, there is no reason at all why we should restrict the term to the written language. Equally the spoken language has a grammar. Indeed there are still hundreds of languages in the world that have no written form yet they all have grammars in the sense in which we are interested in the term.

All too often people tend to think of the spoken language as a rather poor version of the written language. In pronunciation, for example, if someone is in doubt he is likely to appeal to the spelling. Often, in fact, in English the spelling is invoked against the normal usage. They will say 'Well, we pronounce it that way but really it is . . .' I have heard this with the word *omelette*: 'We pronounce it "omelitte" [ɔmlit] but it is really "omelette" [ɔmlet]' (the square brackets indicate a phonetic transcription). We are all accustomed to the idea that English is not pronounced as it is spelt, yet so great is the authority of writing that we can provide a 'correct' pronunciation against the evidence of our own ears. Similarly, people will say that the word *ate* ought to be pronounced to rhyme with *gate* and that in this respect the Scottish pronunciation is correct and the English pronunciation incorrect. People write to the papers complaining about the pronunciation of Montgomery as 'Muntgummery'. They object, too, to the presence of *r* in *Shah of Persia* or the absence of an *r* in *far away* on the grounds that there is or is not an *r* in the spelling. Whether they are or are not right about the acceptability of such forms as standard English is another matter, but they should not argue the point on the grounds of spelling. Moreover, if words are spelt differently, people will simply refuse to believe that they are pronounced in the same way. Many people (not all) make no distinction in speech between *mints* and *mince* or *patients* and *patience*, yet they will insist that they are different because the former of each pair 'has a *t* in it'. Greater incredulity or even hostility will meet the assertion that some well-educated people pronounce *tire* and *tower* like *tar*. Of course, not everybody does, nor even the majority of us; yet these pronunciations are to be found and may even be gaining ground. But there is no point in refusing to accept factual statements about this simply because it seems to be contrary to the evidence of the spelling.

A moment's reflection will soon make it clear that speech cannot in any serious sense be derived from writing and cannot therefore depend on it for correctness or non-correctness. Not only did the spoken language precede the written language historically (and even with a language like English only in very recent times has writing been at all widespread), but also every one of us learnt to speak long before we learnt to write. All the patterns of our language were quite firmly established before we went to school, and when we learnt to write we learnt only to put into written symbols what we already knew. If there is priority it is in the spoken, not the written, form of language.

However, it may be objected that speech is ephemeral while writing is permanent, and that speech is full of errors and false starts while writing more correctly follows the rules. The first point is not, I think, relevant. It does not follow that speech has no grammar just because, as soon as they are spoken, our words are lost for ever unless recorded on a tape recorder or other device. There is, however, an implication here that the written form carries the grammar because it, unlike speech, lasts over the centuries. Shakespeare's works for instance are still available today. But this argument would suggest that the grammar must always stay the same, that the grammar of Shakespeare is the same as the grammar of T. S. Eliot. To some degree this may be so, but it is no more obviously true (or false) of Shakespeare's and Eliot's writing than it is of Shakespeare's and Eliot's speech. The only difference is that because the written records survive we are in a position to compare their written texts but not their speech. It is also true that the written language changes more slowly than the spoken and that it is therefore always more archaic, but this too is not an argument for the suggestion that it and it alone contains the grammar. There is yet a further point: the written language is often far more homogeneous than the spoken. Because it is the language of education it tends to be the same all over the country, whereas the spoken language differs and is represented by many dialects. But this is equally irrelevant. All it could possibly imply would be that there was only one grammar for the whole of, say, the written English language for 300 years over the whole of Britain and the U.S.A., but a lot of different grammars for the spoken language. I do not in fact believe this would be a fair statement of the facts, but even if it were, it would not seriously suggest that grammar was to be found only in the written language.

In many ways, moreover, the written language is a far worse vehicle of communication than the spoken. If we take the number of letters of the alphabet used for English, we find they are insufficient to represent all the possible pronunciations (if we decided to reform the spelling, we should have to invent some new symbols). For instance, English has six 'short' or 'non-final' vowels (i.e. vowel sounds that do not occur at the end of words), but only five vowel symbols *a*, *e*, *i*, *o* and *u*. What happens then when we have a contrast of all six? If we look at English monosyllabic words we can find only two sets of words with all six possibilities:

pit	*rick*
pet	*wreck*
pat	*rack, wrack*
pot	*rock*
putt	*ruck*
put	*rook*

Of particular interest are the devices used to distinguish the last two of each of the set. In the first we write a double *t* for *putt*; in the second we use the symbol *oo* for *rook*.

Much more striking is the failure of the written language to carry much of English intonation. If, for instance, I say *She's very pretty* with a final rising or falling intonation I make a bald statement, but if I use a falling–rising intonation on the last word, I am saying 'She's very pretty, but . . .', leaving it to my hearer to infer what reservations I have. This cannot be represented at all in the written language. Yet it is an essential part of the language and even, perhaps, of the grammar. We may compare the use of a rising intonation for *She's pretty?* and the alternative *Is she pretty?* In the second of these there is a grammatical device that changes the order of the words to form the question. The intonation has a similar function, but it is a moot point whether this too should be regarded as a matter of grammar.

Intonation can, of course, mark grammatical distinctions that are also marked by punctuation. There is a difference in intonation between such phrases as:

> *She speaks French, naturally.*
> *She speaks French naturally.*
> *My brother, who is in London*
> *My brother who is in London*
> *Do you like coffee, or tea?*
> *Do you like coffee or tea?*

This shows that intonation is often a mark of a grammatical distinction that is made in writing. But we do not have to conclude that grammatical distinctions rest solely upon the written form. Precisely what the distinctions are and how we account for them is a different and difficult matter, but they are just as relevant for speech as for writing, and are often to be found in speech alone.

There are many differences between a spoken and a written language. Some are obvious and some are due directly to the difference of the media of sounds versus symbols. I do not intend to discuss here such notorious misfits as *-ough* in *cough, tough, though, bough, through, thought* and *thorough*. But let us look instead at some grammatical differences. We cannot consider syntax in any detail, as it is by no means easy to show any clear-cut differences, but there is one example which is interesting. In written English we would normally wish to avoid *I only saw John* because we do not know whether it means 'All I did was to see John' or 'John was the only one I saw.' Moreover, we should usually be told that the sentence could not have the second of these two meanings; for that, we ought to write *I saw John only*. But none of these considerations is at all valid for spoken English. There is no ambiguity since the intonation shows quite clearly whether we mean *only saw* or *only . . . John*. In the written language there are reasons for arguing that *only* should be placed next to the word it modifies; in the spoken language there are no such reasons, because the intonation clearly indicates with which it is to be linked.

Turning to morphological (inflectional) characteristics we find quite striking differences between the spoken and the written language. In the English number system, for example, there are three common ways of deriving plurals from singulars:

(1) add *-s*   *cat, cats*
(2) 'zero' ending   *sheep, sheep*
(3) change the vowel   *mouse, mice*

All these plurals are found in the spoken language; in fact the same words would be examples. But there are some words which belong to different types in the two forms of the language. For instance, in the written language *postman/postmen* belongs to (3) along with *mouse/mice*. In speech, however, it belongs to (2) with *sheep/sheep* since the spoken form is identical in both cases. If we say

The postman came up the street.

there is nothing to show that it is different from

The postmen came up the street.

How many postmen? One or more than one? We do not know; the form is the same, phonetically [pousmən], in both cases. Of course we can provide a pronunciation that makes the difference, a 'spelling' pronunciation; but such a pronunciation is an artificial one used only when there is pressure to resolve ambiguity. To point to this when discussing the spoken form is cheating – it is assuming that the speech must reflect the writing, and with that assumption, of course, the spoken language cannot have a different grammar.

Another example is to be found in the plural of *house*. In the written language it is regular – *houses*. But in speech it is irregular since the last consonant phonetically [s] is replaced by [z] before the added ending. It is [hauziz] and not [hausiz]. No other word in the English language is exactly parallel; other words with a final [s] do not replace it with [z] in the plural, e.g. *face, horse, lease, moose*, etc. (If in fact we had a similar plural for *face, faces* would be pronounced exactly as *phases*.) All these retain the [s] in the plural while *house* has a change to [z]. The nearest feature to this is found in *wife/wives*, *knife/knives*, *wreath/wreaths*, etc., all of which involve changing a voiceless final consonant (one made without vibration of the vocal cords) in the singular for a voiced consonant (one made with vibration of the vocal cords) in the plural, [f] vs. [v] and [θ] vs. [ð]. The [s]/[z] contrast is similarly one of voiceless and voiced consonants, but this particular contrast is otherwise unknown for the singular/plural relation. Note that the writing indicates the difference between *f* and *v* in the examples quoted, but it does not always do so, for instance in many people's pronunciation of *roofs* (which could have been, but is not, written as *rooves). But the *th* distinction as in *wreath/wreaths* is never made because English has only one way of representing these two different sounds.

There are other examples in the English verb. There is nothing irregular about *does* in the written form. It is exactly parallel with *goes* – *do/does*, *go/goes*. But in speech the form is quite irregular – it is [dʌz]. We find, in fact, that the auxiliary verbs of English, BE, WILL, SHALL, CAN, MUST, etc., have plenty of irregular forms, though not all of them are irregular in the written form. Thus the negative *won't*, *shan't*, *can't* are irregularly formed from *will*, *shall* and *can*, but there is nothing irregular about *mustn't*. But in speech it is irregular since [t] is omitted in the negative – [mʌsnt] not [*mʌstnt]. Most of the auxiliary verbs have irregular -*s* forms ('third person singular') in both speech and writing – *is*, *has*, *does*, *can* (not *cans), *will* (not *wills), etc. There is just one verb in English that has an irregular -*s* form, yet is never an auxiliary but always a main verb. I have asked English people many times to tell me which one this is and seldom do I get an answer, so ignorant are we all of the grammar of our own language. The answer is the verb SAY whose -*s* form *says* is [sez] and not [*seiz]. Strangely enough comic writers use the form *sez* as in '*Sez 'e*' to indicate a substandard form, yet it is a fair representation of a completely normal standard form.

In French we find considerable differences in the forms of written and spoken languages. A striking example is to be found in the feminine forms of the adjectives. The rule in the written language is to add an -*e* to form the feminine. In the spoken form the difference consists of the presence of a consonant in the feminine that is absent in the masculine:

vert	verte	vɛr	vɛrt	'green'
grand	grande	grɑ̃	grɑ̃d	'big'
gris	grise	gri	griz	'grey'
long	longue	lɔ̃	lɔ̃g	'long'

It might at first seem necessary to say that a consonant is added
to the masculine to form the feminine. But the consonant that is
added varies from word to word. There is a much better solution:
the masculine is formed from the feminine by deleting the final
consonant. This may seem a novel way of treating these forms,
but it is clearly the simplest (see pp. 104–5).

In these examples there is at least parallelism. We add an -*e*
to the feminine in the written and delete the final consonant in
the masculine in the spoken. But for other words the two systems
are quite 'out of phase'. Sometimes the writing makes a
distinction that the spoken form does not:

| fier | fière | fjɛr | fjɛr | 'proud' |
| grec | grecque | grɛk | grɛk | 'Greek' |

Sometimes the spoken form has a different consonant:

| neuf | neuve | nœf | nœv | 'new' |
| etc. | | | | |

Of course, people will try to explain the spoken form in terms
of the written, and say for instance that 'the final *e* shows that
the consonant must be pronounced'. But this is nonsense except
as a hint about the way to read written French. In the spoken
form there is no final consonant except in the feminine. It is
always pronounced when it is there, and if it is not there, as in
the masculine, it is neither pronounced nor 'silent'! Moreover,
how could such a statement be true of a native French speaker?
He knew how to form the masculine and feminine forms of the
adjective before he learnt to write them down. It would make
nonsense, therefore, to account for the spoken grammar in terms
of the written. The reverse might be possible, but even that is
misleading. They are two different grammars, though they have
many parallel features.

One moral that might be drawn from all this is that English
and French would be better languages if they reformed their
writing to correspond with speech. But from the point of view of
grammar this would be most unfortunate, for the written
grammar is in many respects simpler than the spoken (not always

– the French verb has far too many endings). For instance, the French device of an -*e* for the feminine ending is simpler than the spoken device of deleting the final consonant, because a deleted consonant cannot be 'recovered'. That is to say if we hear the masculine form we cannot predict the feminine (though this does not really matter for the Frenchman, who knows them both very well). But in the writing we can predict, often at least, both from feminine to masculine and vice versa. Another example comes from English. In the written language we form *photography* and *photographic* from *photograph* by adding endings. In speech we change the whole of the vowel system – [fətɔgrəfi, foutəgræfik, foutəgraːf]. The writing again is more convenient; it indicates a basic or 'underlying' form that does not exist in speech, but one that, as grammarians, we can reconstruct. In this way writing often clarifies important grammatical features of speech. This might be an additional reason for thinking that writing is 'more grammatical'. But the truth of this depends on what is meant by 'grammatical'. Writing is 'more grammatical' in the sense that it often indicates grammatical relationships more clearly, as in the example quoted. It does not, of course, follow that it is 'more grammatical' in the sense of being more correct.

1.5 Form and meaning

Another of the misconceptions that we discussed is that grammar is essentially concerned with meaning. In linguistics, however, we draw a distinction between grammar and semantics (the study of meaning) and insist that they are not identified.

It is easy enough to show that grammatical distinctions are not semantic ones by indicating the many cases where there is not a one-to-one correspondence. An often quoted example is that of *oats* and *wheat*. The former is clearly plural and the latter singular. This is partly indicated by the ending -*s* (though this is not an unambiguous sign of the plural in view of a word like *news* which is singular) but is clearly shown by the fact that we say *The oats are* . . ., *The wheat is* . . . We cannot, however, say in all seriousness that *oats* are 'more than one' while *wheat* is 'one', the traditional definitions of singular and plural. Some people might say that this is true of English at least, but that is only to say that *oats* is grammatically plural and *wheat* grammatically singular. If these people go on to insist that the English think of *oats* as plural and of *wheat* as singular, then this has to be rejected as simply false. Further examples are to be found in *foliage* vs. *leaves*, in English *hair*, which is singular, vs. French *cheveux*, plural. These distinctions are grammatical and do not directly correspond to any categories of meaning. An old joke emphasizes this point:

TEACHER: Is 'trousers' singular or plural?
JOHNNY: Please, Sir, singular at the top and plural at the bottom.

There is then no clear one-to-one relation between the grammatical categories of singular and plural and counting in terms of 'one' and 'more than one'. Nevertheless, in general, there is some correlation between the grammatical distinction and meaning; if there were not, there would be no motivation for the use of the terms 'singular' and 'plural'. But we should say no more than that, in a language in which the grammatical category plural is recognized, it typically, but not by definition, refers to 'more than one'.

The same kind of considerations hold for sex and gender. The Romance languages, especially French, provide examples of this. First, in these languages every noun is either masculine or feminine, e.g. French *le livre* (masculine) 'the book', *la porte* (feminine) 'the door'. Similarly in Italian we find *il libro, la porta*, Spanish *el libro, la puerta*. The similarity of these forms with their genders is a result of their common relationship with the 'parent' language Latin (though Latin has a third gender, neuter). It would make nonsense, however, to say that French, Italian and Spanish people think of all objects as male or female. They do not; it is simply that the grammar of their language divides all nouns into two classes. The essential characteristic of the classification is that members of each class are accompanied by different forms of their article, and of adjectives – *le livre vert, la porte verte* 'the green book', 'the green door'. The irrelevance of any kind of meaning to gender is further illustrated by comparing the genders of words in one language with those in another. A well-known comparison is the gender of the words for 'sun' and 'moon' in the Romance languages and in German. In the Romance languages 'sun' is masculine and 'moon' feminine (French *le soleil, la lune*, Italian *il sole, la luna*, Spanish *el sol, la luna*), but in German 'sun' is feminine and 'moon' masculine (*die Sonne, der Mond*).

A second point is that there are plenty of nouns which, though feminine, normally refer to men, e.g. French *la sentinelle* 'the sentinel', *la vigie* 'the night watchman', *la recru* 'the recruit'. Indeed, most of these names of occupation are feminine even though the person referred to is often a strapping young man. In German there is an even more striking situation. German has three genders – masculine, feminine and neuter – *der Tisch* (masculine) 'the table', *die Tür* (feminine) 'the door', *das Feuer* (neuter) 'the fire', but the two words commonly used to refer to girls and young ladies are neuter – *das Mädchen* and *das Fräulein*! Mark Twain makes use of this confusion of gender and sex in his *A Tramp Abroad*:

GRETCHEN: Wilhelm, where is the turnip?
WILHELM: She has gone to the kitchen.
GRETCHEN: Where is the accomplished and beautiful English maiden?
WILHELM: It has gone to the opera.

Thirdly, adjectives indicating sex often occur with nouns of the 'opposite' gender. In French, 'the mouse' is *la souris* and 'the he-mouse' is *la souris mâle* – 'the male (feminine) mouse'! In Latin, similarly, though *lupus* (masculine) is 'a wolf', the feminine *lupa* is not usually 'she-wolf'. 'She-wolf' is *lupus femina*, while *lupa* is 'a prostitute'. But there is nothing odd about this provided we do not identify grammatical gender with biological sex.

It is not true, of course, that gender has nothing at all to do with sex in the European languages. For most creatures that are obviously male or female the words will normally be masculine and feminine respectively. Thus *l'homme* 'the man' is masculine and *la femme* 'the woman' is feminine (cf. Italian *l'uomo*, *la donna*, Spanish *el hombre*, *la mujer*). It is possible, perhaps even likely, that there is a historical link between gender and sex, in that gender categories may have originated in the 'ancestral' forms of the language as indicators of sex. But as gender has become a formal grammatical category, the link has become very tenuous indeed.

In English there is no gender in this sense at all, no grammatical gender. We have words that refer to male and female creatures – *bull/cow*, *ram/ewe*, *boar/sow* etc. – but this is not a matter of grammar, and should be dealt with in the lexicon or dictionary. If we include this in grammar, we ought also to find a place there for the names of the baby creatures – *calf*, *lamb*, *piglet* – for the language makes a distinction between young and adult in just

the same way as it does between male and female, and there is
no obvious reason why the one should be thought grammatical
but not the other. The traditional grammarians have dealt only
with sex distinctions, but the reason is all too obvious: gender is
assumed to be a characteristic of all languages because it is
found in Latin, but Latin has no grammatical category relating
to the distinction of young and adult. There are also some words
in English which differ in form in terms of a sex relationship,
especially in the ending *–ess*: *author*, *authoress*; *tiger*, *tigress*;
duke, *duchess*. Is this not perhaps gender? The answer again
must be 'no'. It is not enough to have different endings for the
pair of words, they must also involve grammatical features of a
syntactic nature, restrictional features (see pp. 90–98). In the
Romance languages, gender determines the form of the article
and the adjectives, but there is no similar feature in English. If
endings alone were sufficient, then again we ought to ask for a
similar treatment for *pig/piglet*; *duck/duckling*; *goose/gosling*.
This is a noteworthy feature of the English language but it is not
gender.

Yet, no doubt, some will still insist that English has gender.
What about *he/she/it*, *him/her/it*, *his/her/its*? The answer is that
these are used for sex reference, and for precisely this reason
there is no need to talk about gender. Not only do we say

> *The man has left his food,*
> *The woman has left her food,*

but also

> *The cat has left his food,*
> *The cat has left her food,*

according to whether we are talking about a tom-cat or a she-
cat.

The choice of the pronoun, that is to say, depends directly on
the sex of the creature referred to, and there is, therefore,
nothing more that has to be said in the grammar. It is, of course,
true that ships are sometimes referred to as *she*, and so sometimes
are cars and engines. But there is no rule, and it would not be
reasonable to postulate a grammatical category on this evidence
alone. A further point is that the noun/pronoun relation does
not involve a clear restriction – we can say *The girl lost her hat*
or *The girl lost his hat*. The choice depends on the meaning.
With *himself* or *herself*, however, there are strict restrictions –

The girl washed herself, not ... *himself* – and here alone we might seem to be within the province of grammar (see pp. 58–9, 163–4, 188).

It is interesting to note, furthermore, that the close relationship between grammar and sex is largely restricted to languages with which scholars are most familiar, those of the Indo-European and Semitic groups. In other languages, especially in Africa, gender in a strict grammatical sense has nothing to do with sex, but is concerned with the distinction between living and non-living creatures and even between big and small (see p. 81).

Less obvious than the distinction between gender and sex is that between tense and time. Most European languages have special forms of the verb to mark tense – past, present and future. But it would be a mistake to think in terms of some universal characteristic of time markers in the verb. In English the position is rather complex and will therefore be discussed later when we deal in detail with English tense (pp. 198–200), but two points may be made here. First, if the English past tense refers to past time why do we say

If I knew, I would tell you,
or   *I wish I knew*?

The form *knew* is the past tense form of the verb *know*, cf. *I know it now* and *I knew it all yesterday*. But we use the past tense forms of the verb in the two constructions illustrated above, cf. also *if I loved*, *if I went*, *I wish I had*, etc. There is an escape: we say these are not really past tense forms – they are subjunctives or something like that. But this is cheating. It is like pretending that stealing is not a crime by calling it borrowing, a pure terminological trick. The simple fact is that the past tense form does not always refer to past time. Secondly, if we recognize tense wherever we have time relations, why not talk about tense in the noun too? It has been suggested that in that case *fiancée* is future tense, *ex-wife* past tense and *grandfather* pluperfect!

Finally, in this section, we should look at the traditional approach to the definition of the parts of speech, since it too is partly at least in notional terms. For instance, Nesfield defines a noun as 'A word used for naming anything' and notes that 'thing' in the definition stands for person, place, quality, action, feeling, collection, etc.! This is clearly a notional definition at its worst. For how do we know what a thing is? Is fire a thing? Is peace? Is hope or intention? Moreover, can we not say that *red* is the name of a colour and is not *red* then a noun? Nesfield talks about qualities as things, but one would normally think that the words for qualities were adjectives – *brave*, *foolish*, *good*, etc. In fact, the definition is completely vacuous as we can see if we ask how on the basis of this definition can we find the nouns in *He suffered terribly* and *His suffering was terrible*? Is there any sense in which the last sentence has reference to things in a way in which the first does not? For these sentences are identical in meaning. Of course we can say that 'suffering' is a noun and that in this sentence it refers to a thing, the act of suffering being 'treated' as a thing, but this is arguing back to front.

How can we possibly identify 'thing'? There is an easy answer. We do so by using an article or such words as *his*, *this*, in front of the words – *the fire*, *the suffering*, *the place* – and by making them the subject of the sentence. But this is to say that we identify 'things' by looking for the grammatical characteristics of nouns. In other words 'things' are identified by being referred to by nouns. A definition, then, of nouns in terms of things is completely circular. There is no confusion of semantics and grammar this time, merely a failure to recognize that there is no clearly identifiable independent criterion of 'thing'.

The whole of this section is aimed at showing that grammatical categories must be grammatical and not semantic. But we must not overstate the case. There are two reservations to be made. First, we shall often find correlation between grammatical and semantic categories, e.g. between gender and sex, number and counting. This is not surprising, for grammar has a job to do; it would be more surprising if it bore no relation at all to our every-day needs and experience. But it should not be identified with semantics, and we need not expect any one-to-one correlation. Secondly, as linguists we must write our grammars in such a way that they relate to semantics as well as to phonetics – our grammar must be 'sensitive' to semantics. This needs to be said because there was once a strong school of thought that advocated 'formal grammar' (see p. 100), i.e. grammar that is based exclusively on (phonetic and phonological) form. This was far too extreme a requirement. It turned out to be quite unworkable in any

case; no one ever succeeded in writing a grammar that paid
no attention at all to features of meaning. Moreover, would
we want such a grammar? Is not the whole purpose of
describing a language to relate sounds to meaning? Formal
grammar was certainly useful, however, as a reaction against
older, notional views of grammar.

2 Some Traditional Concepts

Traditional grammars make use of a fairly wide technical vocabulary to describe the concepts they use – words like 'noun', 'verb', 'agreement', 'plural', 'clause' and even 'word' itself. Some of the terms are probably unintelligible to most people, though they may have some dim recollection of them from their schooldays. Others would be more familiar – most people would know, or think they know, what is meant by 'plural' or 'noun' and everyone, I suspect, would be convinced that he knew what a word was. However, we cannot take even this for granted. We must look at both the familiar and the less familiar terms to see precisely how they are used and to ask whether their use is really justified. Unfortunately, the usual practice in the grammar is to give some kind of definition of most of the words, but never to question the whole justification of their use.

In this chapter I shall first explain how some of the more important terms have been used in the past, but secondly, and more importantly, discuss the value of some of the concepts and the ways in which they can be or have been used in more recent studies of linguistics.

2.1 Words

In literate societies, at least, the word is so much a part of everyday knowledge that it is completely taken for granted. Grammar books often make no attempt to give a definition of the word though they happily define other grammatical elements in terms of it. The sentence, for instance, is a 'combination of words' and the parts of speech are 'classes of words'. But what a word is and how it can be defined is often not considered.

The chief reason for this is that in the written language there is no doubt at all about the status of the word. Words are clearly identified by the spaces between them. On any page of print we can simply count how many words there are by counting the groups of letters that are separated by spaces. Moreover, with

41

one or two exceptions, which are mostly concerned with hyphens, everyone knows just where to put the spaces. (Exceptions are of the kind *well-chosen* or *well chosen* or perhaps even *wellchosen*.) The word is part of our writing conventions and we learn what words are when we first learn to spell. The placing of the spaces is as much a part of our education and is as well established as spelling and punctuation, perhaps more so than the latter.

However, we are not concerned only with writing, but also with speech. Are there, similarly, words in the spoken language? It is not easy to give a direct answer to this question. There are three points that we should consider.

First, we must not simply project the written word on to the spoken word. That is, we must not assume that wherever we have words in writing we must have words in speech. This is a clear example of one of the areas in language study in which we must keep speech and writing distinct, even if it is very difficult to do so. After an education that has been largely in terms of the written word the average person finds it very difficult to question the universally held assumption that there are words in the spoken language too. But if we are to look at language objectively we must question this assumption.

Secondly, it is a fact that there are no spaces between 'words' in speech. This comes as a surprise to many people. So great is the influence of writing that they actually 'hear' in speech what they see in writing. Even some grammarians have made this mistake. They have been misled by a false parallelism between speech and writing and have assumed that there are slight pauses between words. This point can be proved quite easily by carefully listening to people speaking – there are no breaks between the 'words'. What breaks there are, come at the end of groups of 'words' – phrases, clauses, sentences. This is borne out, too, by experimental phonetics. Any kind of visual representation of speech by mechanical or electronic instruments (and there are many kinds) shows speech as a continuum without any breaks at the points where the written words would be divided. More convincingly, perhaps, if we listen to an unfamiliar language we find it quite impossible to divide up the speech into any kind of limited stretches except those marked by pauses and by intonation, but these are always very much larger than single words. Clearly, recognizing the word in speech is not a matter of detecting breaks in the stream of speech, for there are no breaks to detect. There are, however, as we shall see later in this chapter, some features that mark off stretches of speech that partially at least (and in different ways in different languages) correspond to the words of the written language.

Thirdly, it is highly probable that the words of the written language are not purely conventional. They more likely correspond to some kind of linguistically justified unit. That is, we should expect to find that there are some principles underlying word division. It would otherwise be extremely difficult for the child to learn the rules for written word division and even highly educated adults could be expected to make far more mistakes than they actually do. Moreover, it is said that even in non-literate societies there is a clear recognition of the word – that the word is 'institutionalized'. I am not sure that this is very significant, for its relevance will depend on what is meant by 'clear recognition'. It may well mean no more than that linguists are able, on the basis of the linguistic behaviour of these people, to establish the words of the language (by methods of the kind we shall soon be considering). It is all too easy to see as linguistic realities those linguistic entities that we wish to establish in order to undertake our description of the language. There is, furthermore, some quite good evidence that the word is not a natural linguistic entity. We have only to look at ancient inscriptions to see this. The use of spaces to indicate word division belongs to Roman times; the Greeks did not use spaces, but ran all their words together. But we would be on dangerous ground if we said the Greeks had no notion of the word, for the whole of one work of the Greek philosopher Plato, the *Cratylus*, is about language, and is largely centred upon items that are unmistakably words.

We have to ask ourselves, then, quite objectively, what a word is, how it can be defined and even perhaps whether there are words in the spoken language. There have been three main approaches to this problem. The first is to see the word as a semantic unit, a unit of meaning; the second sees it as a phonetic or phonological unit, one that is marked, if not by 'spaces' or pauses, at least by some features of the sounds of the language; the third attempts to establish the word by a variety of linguistic procedures that are associated with the idea that the word is in some ways an isolable and indivisible unit.

Let us begin by looking at semantic definitions of the word. In fact these are not so much semantic as notional, and fail for all the reasons we have already discussed in dealing with form and meaning. The word is said to be a linguistic unit that has a single meaning. The difficulty, of course, is in deciding what is meant by a single meaning, for meanings are even less easy to identify than words. It is easy enough to show in a variety of ways that we cannot define words in terms of units of meaning. To begin with, it is very clear that very many single words cover not one but two or more 'bits' of meaning. If *sing* has a single meaning, then presumably *singer* has more since it means *one who sings* and even *sang* must mean both *sing* and 'past time'. Similarly, we can hardly say that *lamb*, *ewe* and *ram* have single meanings since they all mean 'sheep', but 'baby', 'mother' and 'father' as well. It is, moreover, a pure accident whether we use one or two words to describe the baby, the female or the male of any species. Alongside *lamb*, *ewe* and *ram* we have *elephant calf*, *elephant cow* and *elephant bull*. The reason for the difference is obvious – we are less familiar in our culture (or at least our ancestors were less familiar) with elephants than with sheep – but that proves nothing about the amount of meaning in one word. Even with objects that are more familiar to modern society there are similar discrepancies. We have to use two words to distinguish *passenger train* from *goods train*, though for a similar distinction with road vehicles we have *bus* and *lorry*. The point is stressed further if we look at other languages. The Eskimo has four words for different kinds of snow, the Bedouin has many words for all the different kinds of camel that he recognizes. To translate these into English we have to use more than one word.

Conversely, it is not always possible to assign a meaning or a set of meanings to a single word; the semantic unit is a sequence of several words. The meaning of *put up with* ('tolerate'), for instance, cannot be stated in terms of the individual meanings of *put*, *up* and *with*, but has to be stated for the whole combination. There are many sequences of this kind in English – *make up*, *take to*, *look for*, *put off*, *take in*, etc. These are usually called 'phrasal verbs', but the relevant point about them is that they are idioms, expressions whose meaning cannot be derived from the meaning of the individual words.

Yet a further point about the relation of word to meaning arises from the fact that very often word division does not appear to correspond to meaning division. For instance, we cannot divide *heavy smoker* into *heavy* and *smoker* if we are thinking in terms of meaning, for a heavy smoker is not both a smoker and heavy. Other examples are *artificial florist* and *criminal lawyer*. In these, division into meaningful elements would seem to be, not at word division, but within the second word – *heavy smok/er, artificial flor/ist, criminal law/yer*. Clearly the word cannot be defined as a unit of meaning.

Let us next consider phonetic and phonological definitions of the word. Some languages have vowel harmony, in which sequences of vowels must be alike in terms of some phonetic feature – of openness/closeness, frontness/backness, rounding/unrounding (the first two refer to positions of the tongue, the last to the shape of the lips). This feature is often, but not always, a characteristic of the word. Thus in Turkish all the vowels of a word must be either front or back and either unrounded or rounded:

ev	'house'	*evim*	'my house'	(front, unrounded)
göz	'eye'	*gözüm*	'my eye'	(front, rounded)
yol	'way'	*yolum*	'my way'	(back, rounded)
kız	'daughter'	*kızım*	'my daughter'	(back, unrounded).

Other languages have 'fixed stress', i.e. the stress always falls on a particular syllable of a word, perhaps the first or the last, or perhaps on different syllables according to the structure of the word. But it is always predictable, whereas it is not predictable in English (or Russian), so that it is always possible to determine from the stress where a word begins or ends.

English has nothing quite like this, but there are two features that are associated with the word. The first is stress; what we may call 'full' stress, though not placed on any particular syllable, nevertheless falls on only one syllable in each word. By this means we can argue that *blackbird, blackboard, greenhouse*, are single words whereas *black bird, black board, green house* are two. Unfortunately, there is no consistent relation between stress patterns and our writing conventions. *The White House*, for instance, is pronounced as if *White House* were one word and we may compare (all with a single stress) *table top, cushion cover, shoe polish* with *beehive, cowshed, birdcage*. Moreover, some little words with an essentially grammatical function are usually unstressed and belong to the stress pattern of a preceding or following word. Thus *beat her* is often pronounced in exactly the same way as *beater* and *kissed her* rhymes with *sister* as we know from 'O my Darling Clementine'. Some linguists have, indeed, regarded these as 'phonological' words.

English also has what is commonly known as 'juncture'. This is illustrated by the fact that even in normal speech it is possible to distinguish between:

that stuff	*that's tough*
a nice cake	*an ice cake*
keep sticking	*keeps ticking*
grey day	*Grade A*

The vowels and consonants of each pair are identical. How, then, do they differ? They are said to differ in juncture. The precise signal for this distinction varies – in the case of the third pair the noticeable feature is the aspiration (the 'h'-like sound) that follows the articulation of the *t* of *ticking*, and elsewhere it is largely a matter of the timing of the various articulatory movements. What is important here is not the precise phonetics, but the fact that it is clear that we can distinguish the pairs. We have, it follows, marks of word division since we can distinguish between two utterances that are otherwise identical. Unfortunately, word division is not always signalled by juncture, for although the first two syllables of *a tack* and *at Acton* are different, there is no difference between *a tack* and *attack*. Here juncture allows us to distinguish between two sequences of words that are divided differently, but not between the first of these sequences and the single word. Similarly in *the potato* there is no way of showing that the division is between *the* and *potato* rather than between *the po-* and *-tato*, though we know it is not between *the pot-* and *-ato* for exactly the same reasons as those that allow us to distinguish *attack* and *a tack* from *at Acton*. Moreover, for many people *at all* is pronounced as if it were *a tall* – in other words the juncture feature suggests the wrong word division. The reason here is that *at all* is treated as if it were a single word like *nearly*, *wholly*, etc.; as a single word it would be phonetically identical with *a tall*.

We must ask, however, whether this is really relevant. Even if we had clear features of sound marking off words, would they then define words or should we look elsewhere for the definition? Phonetic definitions of the word are, perhaps, as irrelevant as semantic ones – the word ought to be definable as a grammatical unit? We may be thankful that we have clues to word division, but the clues are not part of the criteria. This leads on to the third kind of approach (see p. 43) to the definition of the word. A simple and plausible definition is in terms not of pause, but of potential pause. We can establish words by asking where we can pause if we so wish. So we know that there are three words *I saw John* because we can divide by pausing, into *I* and *saw John*, and *I saw* and *John*. But this is unsatisfactory because we almost certainly pause where we know the spaces would come in the writing. This then merely takes over the written word by allowing potential pause wherever there are spaces. Moreover is it really true that we can only pause between words? Surely we can pause, in deliberate speech, between the parts of *postman*, *sleepless* and even *discuss* and *consider*. We can even invent situations in which we can divide speech into syllables or even into letter-sounds, *c - a - t*. Do these then become words?

There are similar difficulties with any definition of the word as an 'indivisible unit'. It is sometimes suggested, for instance, that a word is a linguistic unit which does not permit the insertion of any other linguistic material. For instance, we know that *little boy* is two words because we can insert *English* – *little English boy* – but we cannot insert anything within, say, *singing*. But this too turns out to be false for we can divide *singing* into two parts *sing-* and *-ing*, and insert *-ing and danc-* to give us *singing and dancing*. Of course we did not insert a word or even whole words, but that is no objection. If we have not yet established what a word is we cannot require that the 'no insertion' criterion applies only to complete words!

A famous definition of the word that suffers from the same defects is that of the great American linguist Leonard Bloomfield. He defined a word as a 'minimum free form'. What he meant was the smallest bit of speech that can occur in isolation. But again what we are prepared to utter in isolation is almost certainly what we have learnt to recognize as a word in writing. Certainly many 'words' would not occur by themselves in any natural conversation. We should find it difficult to provide a context for the occurrence in isolation of *the* or *a* or *my* and in French of *à* or *je*, except one in which we were deliberately talking about words, e.g. 'What is the first word in *the book*?' or even the apparently harmless 'What comes before *book* in *the book*?' It is obvious, however, that questions like this, questions about language, cannot fairly be used to establish what words are. First, they assume again that we already know what words are, and secondly we could produce quite bogus words by asking

48 Grammar

for instance 'What comes before *-ject* in *reject*?' (answer '*re*'), or 'What is the last element of *boy's*?' (answer '*s*'), or 'What have *pity* and *intensity* in common?' (answer '*ity*'). In other words, anything can occur in isolation if we want to talk about it. If Bloomfield's test is to be of any use we must restrict our attention to ordinary language and not to language about language. One way out of the difficulty that has been proposed is to say that words like *the*, *a*, *my*, *je*, etc., while not themselves minimum free forms, nevertheless function in essentially the same way as many others that are. *The*, for instance, and *a* are like *this* and *that*, which do occur alone, and French *je* is like *Pierre*. But this does not help, since the English possessive *'s* as in *John's* is like *of*, and the prefix *in-* in *intolerable* is like *not*, but this would not be a good argument for treating them as words. (There is a story about the film producer Sam Goldwyn – a 'Goldwynism' – in which he allegedly said 'I can describe your proposal in just two words – "Im possible!" ') Moreover, some of these forms are not used in isolation because the language has a different form for use there. We have no form in isolation to correspond to *the* and *a*, but we have *mine* and *yours* for *my* and *your*, and French *moi* for *je* and *lui* for *il*. The evidence for these forms suggests, in fact, that the forms that are never used in isolation are not minimum free forms.

In conclusion, sadly, we have to say that the word is not a clearly definable linguistic unit. We shall, perhaps, have to recognize some kind of unit that corresponds closely to the written word and define it ultimately in terms of a combination of the features we have been considering, though as we shall see in the next chapter some theorists have decided to do without the word altogether. But what the word is or is not depends ultimately on our total view of grammar.

2.2 Inflection and syntax

We saw in the last section that traditional grammars treat words as their basic units. There is, however, a further problem about words that we have not yet considered. It is that in many languages words have, or may be said to have, many different forms. In English, for instance, the verb 'to take' is said to have the forms *take*, *takes*, *took*, *taking* and *taken* (and perhaps *taker*). Similarly, the word 'cat' has the two forms *cat* and *cats*.

We have to be careful about our terminology because the

word 'word' is used in two different senses. We talk about the words *cat* and *cats* and at the same time about the word 'cat' which has a singular form *cat* and a plural form *cats*. In the former usage, *cat* and *cats* are different words, while in the latter they are forms of the same word. Obviously we ought to distinguish between words and forms of words. We might talk about the word 'cat' and say that it has two forms *cat* and *cats* so that *cats* is not a word at all, but one form of the word. But this is, of course, to define 'word' in a way quite different from the usage in the previous section. An alternative way of handling the problem is to say that *cat* and *cats* are different words (not just different forms), and to find a new term for 'cat' which covers them both. One suggested term is 'lexeme', but 'lexical item' is better. Whichever alternative we choose we shall restrict the use of 'word' to one or other of the possible meanings. The best way to avoid confusion, however, is not to lay down strict rules about the use of terms but to use a different way of indicating 'words' in each of the two senses. This I have already been doing by using small capital letters for words as lexical items and italics for words as forms of words, e.g. CAT and *cat*, *cats*.[1]

There might seem, perhaps, not to be the same confusion with verbs because we talk about 'the verb "to take"' with its various forms but would not describe 'to take' as a word since it is clearly two. But there is still the problem, because we often speak of the verb 'to take' and also of *takes* as a verb. We want to say that *to take* (as well as *takes* and *take*) is one of the forms of the verb 'to take'. Supposing, for instance, that we say that *kept* cannot be followed by 'to seem', is this meant to imply that we cannot follow *kept* by the form *to seem*, i.e. that there is no **he kept to seem* ... (which is obviously true), or that *kept* cannot be followed by one of the forms of the verb 'to seem', e.g. *seeming*, i.e. that there is no *he kept seeming* ... (which might seem plausible but is almost certainly untrue)? What we need is the distinction between TO SEEM the verb and *to seem* the form of the verb. More strictly, we should say that *to take* is not a form of the verb, but that *take* is. If so, we do not need to refer to the verb TO TAKE, but to the verb TAKE. The choice of TO TAKE as the name for the verb, the so called 'infinitive', is probably based on

1. I shall distinguish between 'words' and 'forms of words' only where there is danger of confusion. Similarly, I shall use small capitals rather than italics only where it is important to stress that we are concerned with words as lexical items. (Small capitals are also used for important technical terms.)

the needs of languages other than English, e.g. French *aimer*, Italian *amare* 'to love'. Not only is TAKE without TO quite sufficient for English, but also we run into difficulties if we try to refer to the auxiliary verbs by a TO ('infinitive') form. A French scholar in fact once referred to the English verbs 'to will' and 'to shall', though of course no such forms exist. And we can have the same kind of fun with the other auxiliaries 'to can', 'to may', 'to must' and 'to ought'. In fact, except for 'to ought', such verbs exist in English, though they are totally unrelated to the auxiliary verbs of English – 'to can' is 'to put into cans', 'to may' is 'to celebrate May day', 'to must' is 'to go musty'. What we must do, of course, is to talk of the auxiliaries WILL, SHALL, CAN, MAY, MUST and OUGHT.

The way in which the verb is referred to in grammar books varies according to the language. For Latin the forms meaning 'I advise', 'I love', etc. are chosen – the form *amo* is used to refer to the verb AMO. For Semitic languages it would be the form meaning 'he loves', for French or Russian the form meaning 'to love'. The form I have chosen for English, *love* (for the verb LOVE), is the 'simple' or 'unmarked' form which is used in a variety of positions where other languages use the 'infinitive' or the 'imperative' or even one of the forms of the present tense. This can be shown by *come* in:

> *I saw him come.*
> *Come here at once.*
> *I come every day.*

Most of the languages with which we are familiar have a far more complex morphology than English. Latin, for instance, has about 120 forms of the verb, beginning, as generations of schoolchildren have learnt, with *amo, amas, amat, amamus, amatis, amant*. But equally French, German, Italian and most other European languages have far more forms than English, which (except with BE) never has more than five different forms of the verb, e.g. *take, takes, taking, took, taken*, and often only three, e.g. *hit, hits, hitting*. Many other languages have highly complex verb morphology, e.g. the Bantu languages such as Nyanja, Kikuyu and Swahili, and many of the American Indian languages.

Some languages have many forms of the noun, though, apart from the possessive forms, English has never more than two, the singular and the plural (unless we count the small number which appear to have two plurals, e.g. *brother*, *brothers*, *brethren*; *index*, *indexes*, *indices*). But Latin nouns have seven or eight different forms. The way that they are set out in the grammar books (in 'paradigms') suggests that there might be twelve different forms, but some of the forms appear more than once, e.g.:

	SINGULAR	PLURAL
nominative	*amicus* ('friend')	*amici*
vocative	*amice*	*amici*
accusative	*amicum*	*amicos*
genitive	*amici*	*amicorum*
dative	*amico*	*amicis*
ablative	*amico*	*amicis*

The Latin adjectives have considerably more forms because adjectives can be masculine, feminine or neuter. The number of forms listed in the paradigms is thirty-six though the number of actually different forms is only fourteen.

Other languages, such as Chinese, as we saw in the first chapter, have no distinct forms of words at all. They have no inflection, no morphology. There are other languages, however, which, though they have many forms of the same word, have a morphology that is very different from that of Latin, French, or even Arabic. In these languages the forms are always made up of clearly identifiable parts. In Swahili, for example, the translation of 'he saw you' is *alikuona*, which seems to be a single word. But it is in fact composed of four parts *a* 'he', *li* past tense, *ku* 'you' and *ona* 'see'. These can be replaced by similar elements, e.g. *ni* for 'I' or 'me', or *ta* for future, so that we can form the words *atakuona* 'he will see you', *nilikuona* 'I saw you', *ataniona* 'he will see me' and so on. All we have to do is to put the correct elements together in the right order. This is very different from Latin where *amo* means 'I love', *amat* 'he loves', *amabam* 'I loved'. There are here no distinct elements for 'I', 'he', present tense or past tense. The term 'inflectional' is used to refer to languages like Latin in which the grammatical elements cannot be separated, while the term for languages like Swahili is 'agglutinative'. There is very little point in writing out paradigms for the Swahili verbs; all we need to do is to list the various elements that make up the word.

The nineteenth-century scholar Wilhelm von Humboldt

divided all the languages of the world into three types – 'inflectional', 'agglutinative' and 'isolating'. As we have seen, Latin and Swahili are examples of inflectional and agglutinative languages respectively. An example of an isolating language is Chinese – or any other language that has no morphology. This is not a very useful classification of languages as a whole, for two reasons. First, it refers only to one aspect of the language, the word formation. Secondly, most languages have characteristics of all three types. Swahili, for instance, is not wholly agglutinative, but has some inflection in the strict sense; a better example of an agglutinative language might be Turkish. Classical Greek was highly inflectional. The -o: of *luo:* 'I loose' identifies no less than five categories – person (first person), number (singular), tense (present), mood (indicative) and voice (active). Nevertheless the form *lusontai*, 'they will loose themselves' can be split into six parts (and so treated as a word in an agglutinative language) – *lu* 'loose', *s* future tense, *o* indicative mood, *n* plural number, *t* third person and *ai* middle or passive voice. In English there are words exhibiting all three types. The prepositions, e.g. *by*, *near*, *to*, are 'invariable' and so might have belonged to an isolating language, *see/saw* is an example of inflection, while the forms *love/loves/loved/loving* could all be handled in terms of agglutination. This division into inflectional, agglutinative and isolating cannot then be a division of language types, but only of the morphological characteristics of parts of languages.

The traditional grammars deal with morphology in what is sometimes called the 'word and paradigm' approach. A single word such as Latin AMO has all its forms set out in lists – paradigms:

amo	'I love'
amas	'thou lovest'
amat	'he loves'
amamus	'we love'
amatis	'you love'
amant	'they love'

and so on, throughout all the tenses, moods and voices of Latin, a sum total of at least 120 forms.

This is not a wholly satisfactory approach because it relies too much on the intuition of the student. For he is merely told that AMO is a 'first conjugation verb', that MONEO 'I advise' is a 'second conjugation verb' and so on, and then is expected to work out for himself the forms of LAUDO 'I praise' on the analogy of AMO. In other words, he is never told precisely what are the forms of the other verbs of Latin; he is left to deduce for himself the points of similarity and difference. What is important, one would have thought, is not the forms of AMO, but the endings of all the verbs of this 'first conjugation'. Moreover, when the pupil learns REGO 'I rule' (third conjugation) and AUDIO 'I hear' (fourth conjugation) he is given a decreasing amount of time to learn them because they differ from AMO in certain fairly clearly establishable ways – partly that where AMO has an -*a*- and MONEO an -*e*-, REGO has various short vowels and AUDIO an -*i*-. The student is not told this; he is left to work it out for himself. This may be good exercise for the brain, but it is not good linguistics. What we need is a precise and explicit statement of the way in which the forms are related to one another, and this we do not find in a 'word and paradigm' grammar. We shall consider some alternatives later.

Grammar is not merely a matter of morphology (see p. 13). It is also concerned with syntax, the way in which words or particular word classes are combined to form larger constructions, and ultimately sentences. Thus it is a matter of syntax that we say *Birds sing* rather than *Sing birds*, that we cannot say *Soon saw happily John* or that *John saw Bill* is different from *Bill saw John*. A little more subtly, the joke about *Time flies* ('You can't – they fly too fast') results from the fact that there are two possible constructions, either noun–verb or verb–noun (because both *time* and *flies* can be either verbs or nouns). A similar example is the headline *British bitter wins in Europe*. Is this about the success of bitter ale or about some unhappy victories in football? It depends on whether *bitter wins* is a noun and a verb or adjective and a noun, whether it is to be compared with *bitter fails* or with *happy wins*. Since these are all matters of syntax it follows that it is unlikely that there are any languages without syntax; and there are, therefore, no languages without grammar. Today syntax receives more attention than morphology; this is reflected in the length of Chapters 4 and 5.

A more specialized type of syntax is that which is concerned with concord and government (see 2.6). This deals with the occurrence in specific linguistic contexts of one form of a word rather than another; of, for instance, *takes* instead of *take* in *He . . . a bath every day*, or of *mensam* or *mensas* rather than any other form of the noun MENSA 'a table' in . . . *videt* 'he sees . . .' This involves morphology as well as syntax, and is the basis for recognizing grammatical categories such as number, gender, case; such categories are MORPHOSYNTACTIC (p. 78). Thus number, singular and plural, in English is defined in terms both of the morphology of the noun and occurrence ('agreement') with specific forms of the verb as in:

> *The cat sits on the mat.*
> *The cats sit on the mat.*

However, these morphosyntactic categories are not involved in all morphological variation. *Catty* is morphologically related to *cat*, and is so treated by the dictionary, but the distinction does not involve concord or government. We may similarly relate *fame* and *famous*, *man* and *manhood*, *serene* and *serenity*, *black* and *blacken*. Relations of this kind are dealt with under DERIVATION. This is usually contrasted with 'inflection', which we were considering previously, but that terminology ignores the fact that even in agglutinative languages there may be a distinction of a similar kind.

Although the defining characteristic of derivation is that no morphosyntactic categories are directly involved, there are other typical features. First, whereas inflectional features involve only one word class (the number/person forms of the verb are all verbs), derivation often (but not always) changes the word class, from noun to verb, from verb to noun, from noun to adjective, etc. Secondly, there is much greater irregularity in both the formal pattern and the meaning relations. The adjectives formed from *fame*, *president*, *man*, *phoneme* and *mass* are *famous*, *presidential*, *manly*, *phonemic*, *massive* – and there are many other types. Similarly, on the semantic side the suffix *-able* has a variety of meanings: *drinkable* is 'that can be drunk', *commendable* 'that should be commended', *readable* 'that can be easily read with pleasure', *lovable* 'that is naturally loved'. Some *-able* words, e.g. *formidable*, cannot be analysed into further elements either morphologically or semantically.

For these reasons the natural place to deal with derivation is in the dictionary. Each word may be included in a section headed by the word treated as basic, and a statement of each form and meaning can be given. By contrast, the dictionary will not give all the inflected forms or their meanings. For that is a matter of grammar.

2.3 Parts of speech

The traditional grammars often began with a statement of the 'parts of speech', which today would be called 'word classes'. According to most grammars there are eight parts of speech. They are (with typical examples):

noun	(*howling, wolf, flock, terror*)
pronoun	(*I, you, he, which*)
adjective	(*this, the, fourth, each, untidy*)
verb	(*see, retire, laugh*)
preposition	(*on, in, to*)
conjunction	(*and, but, because*)
adverb	(*much, deservedly, partly, merely*)
interjection	(*alas*)

This kind of classification goes back to the Greek philosophers Plato and Aristotle, though the first really clear statement comes from the most famous of Greek grammarians, Dionysius Thrax, who produced a grammar of Greek in about 100 B.C. Dionysius also recognized eight parts of speech. Six of them were identical with those listed above; the only difference in the more modern list is that it has distinguished nouns and adjectives and added the interjections, omitting the participle and the article as separate parts of speech. There is little explanation why these parts of speech are chosen for English; they are simply taken over from the classical grammarians. There are, however, serious objections to this classification.

First, the definitions are largely notional and extremely vague. It would often be quite impossible to judge from them whether a particular word was a noun, a verb or an adjective without knowing the answer already! We have discussed Nesfield's definition of a noun on pp. 39–40 and seen how circular it was. His definition of the verb is utterly uninformative – 'a verb is a word used for *saying* something about something else.' Do not most words say something about something else? His definitions of the pronoun and the adjective are a little better: 'A pronoun is a word used instead of a noun', 'An adjective is a word used to qualify a noun.' They are almost definitions in grammatical terms, as they should be, but they are still not precise enough. If we consider the pronoun we can see that many kinds of word may be used instead of the noun *John*:

> *John came this morning.*
> *A man/Someone/You-know-who/The aforementioned came
> this morning.*

In the definition of the adjective what does 'qualify' mean?
Precede? Either precede or follow? Is *John's* an adjective in
John's book or *there* in *the people there*? (See p. 61.) It is
interesting to note that the definitions given by Dionysius Thrax
almost two thousand years ago were formal, based largely upon
morphology (though we may well question whether morphology
ought to determine word classes. For this reason he placed noun
and adjective in the same class, because in Greek both have case
endings.

Secondly, the number of parts of speech in the traditional grammars seems to be quite arbitrary. Why eight? Probably because
Dionysius Thrax had eight. The adverb in particular is a most
peculiar class. It is quite clearly a 'rag bag' or 'dustbin', the class
into which words that do not seem to belong elsewhere are placed.
This is easily illustrated by considering *very* and *quickly*, both of
which are traditionally considered to be adverbs. They have almost
nothing in common, as shown by the following pairs of possible
and impossible sentences (the latter marked with asterisks):

> *He ran away quickly.*
> **He ran away very.*
> *He is very good.*
> **He is quickly good.*
> *He has a very fast car.*
> **He has a quickly fast car.*

We can overcome this problem if we wish by recognizing two
different classes, one of 'adverbs' – *quickly*, *beautifully*, etc. –
and the other of 'intensifiers' – *very*, *fairly*, *quite*, etc. But we are
then faced with the problem of the status of other rather similar
words like *usually*. Is this an adverb in the same (though
restricted sense) in which *quickly* is? Again let us look at some
sentences:

> **He ran away usually* (but *He usually ran away*).
> *He ran away quickly.*
> *He is usually good.*
> **He is quickly good.*
> **He has a usually fast car.*
> **He has a quickly fast car.*

It would appear, then, that we need far more classes than eight. The American scholar C. C. Fries suggested that English had four parts of speech and fifteen groups of 'form words'. The four parts of speech he labelled classes 1, 2, 3 and 4, but they are clearly what would normally be called 'nouns', 'verbs', 'adjectives' and 'adverbs'. Fries was at pains to warn the reader against this identification of his classes with these traditional parts of speech, because he wanted to insist that his theoretical framework was different from that of the traditional grammars. We need not be too concerned about this; there is much to be said for retaining the old terms simply because it is so much easier to remember them, provided we are careful not to forget that we are using them differently. A particularly striking point about Fries's classification is that what traditional grammars call adverbs are treated in no less than five of his fifteen groups as well as providing the total membership of his class 4. The correspondences between the two systems of classification, using Nesfield (p. 27) as an example of a traditional grammarian, are:

FRIES	NESFIELD	EXAMPLE
Class 4	Time	*now*
	Place	*here*
	Number	*once*
	Description	*slowly*
Group C	Affirming or denying	*not*
Group D	Quality, extent or degree	*very*
Group H	Place (introductory)	*there* (*is*/*are* . . .)
Group I	Interrogative	*when*
Group L	Affirming or denying	*no*

There are difficulties with Fries's classification, but at least he showed that the eight traditional parts of speech are not satisfactory.

Word classes are a necessary part of any description of a language. The grammar will be largely stated in terms of their functions, while the lexicon must show to which class each individual word belongs, e.g. that *elephant* is a noun, *depend* is a verb. But the definitions are not independent of the grammar; precisely what a noun is in English, say, will depend on the functions of that class of word in the grammar. The functions may be many and varied. The noun *boy*, for instance, has a different function in each of the following sentences, and the grammar must specify quite clearly what these functions are:

> *The boy has come.*
> *I've seen the boy.*
> *I gave it to the boy.*
> *This is the boy's mother.*

By making quite clear that words such as *boy* have these (and other) functions, the grammar provides a definition of the noun.

Provided we are aware of the problems, we can use the traditional parts of speech and their terminology as the basis for word classification. We can probably recognize nouns and verbs in all languages, though this is less certain of other parts of speech. In English every complete sentence (p. 67) must contain at least one word from each class (if we include, for the moment, pronouns among nouns). Thus, a sentence such as *Birds fly* is the smallest possible (though some languages, e.g. Latin, permit sentences consisting of verbs alone). Apart from the *-er* and *-est* forms of adjectives, only nouns and verbs have morphological features in English. The noun usually has two forms, singular and plural (e.g. *cat*, *cats*), while the verb may have up to five, *take*, *takes*, *took*, *taken* and *taking*, which we may call the simple form, the *-s* form, the past tense form, the past participle, and the present participle or *-ing* form respectively. The most important subclassification of nouns is into countables and uncountables. This accounts for the fact that *book* normally requires *a* before it in the singular, while *butter* cannot occur normally with *a* (see p. 197):

> *There is a book/butter on the table.*
> **There is book/a butter on the table.*

The most important subclassification of the verb is into auxiliaries and full verbs, the auxiliaries being BE, HAVE, DO and the modals WILL, SHALL, CAN, MAY, MUST and OUGHT TO, and to some extent DARE and NEED.

We have so far treated the pronoun as a type of noun. This correctly reflects its major syntactic functions, but it has special characteristics of its own. First, it has different forms relating to person (p. 83) and sex (p. 37). Secondly, the third person pronouns often refer, or corefer (see 5.5), to noun phrases, their antecedents, e.g.:

> *I saw* the old woman *and spoke to* her.

There are two main types of pronoun, the personal pronouns

I/me, you, he/him, she/her, it, we/us, they/them and the reflexives *myself, yourself, himself, herself, itself, yourselves* and *themselves.* The reflexives are generally used for coreference within the same clause, the others for coreference elsewhere. Thus we may distinguish:

He hurt himself/He hurt him.

It is to be noticed that the traditional definition of a pronoun in terms of 'being used instead of a noun' is misleading. It is used 'instead of' a noun phrase as the example above shows; in contrast we cannot say:

*I saw the old woman *and spoke to the silly* her.

(But see 4.3 on this and on the status of *one* in *the old one.*) Moreover, it is not only pronouns that are used 'instead of' other categories. There are several types of PROFORMATION: auxiliary verbs are, perhaps, used as 'pro-verbs', while some adverbs corefer with prepositional phrases:

John hasn't been swimming, *but I* have.
He lives in London, *but his mother has never been* there.

Another major class is the adjective, with two main functions, attributive and predicative, as illustrated by *the little boy* and *The boy is little* respectively. But the traditional term 'adjective' includes words that are best regarded as members of a different class. The articles (*the, a*), possessive pronouns (*his, her, my, their,* etc.), demonstratives (*this, that, these, those*), plus words such as *all, some, neither,* which precede the adjectives proper and most of which are never used predicatively, are treated today as 'determinatives' or 'determiners'.

The adverb we have already discussed. The preposition functions with a noun or rather a noun phrase (see p. 70) as in *to John, on the table,* with the resulting sequence of words functioning like an adverb of time or place. Finally, conjunctions are words that link sentences, though we should, perhaps, distinguish those that coordinate and those that subordinate (see p. 72).

This does not account for all words of English. There are others such as *not, who, yes,* that have very special functions and belong either to a class of their own or to a class with very few members. It was for this reason that Fries distinguished between parts of speech and form words, or, as other scholars have called them, 'full' words and 'empty' words, or 'lexical' and 'grammatical' words. The form words include not only words such as these, but also pronouns and determiners and, perhaps, conjunctions and even prepositions. The distinction is a useful one in that the form words belong to a limited 'closed' class that can be listed, and so dealt with in the grammar, whereas the full words are members of an 'open' set which is unlimited or indefinite in number, and so more appropriately left to the dictionary. But there is no very precise line of division between them.

Even on this approach, however, several problems arise. The first results from the fact that some word classes have a variety of functions, but, unfortunately, not all words of the class seem to have all the functions. This problem is well illustrated by the adjective. It will be remembered that we spoke of its attributive and predicative functions as in *the little boy* and *The boy is little*. But there are words that may be used predicatively but not attributively. Examples are *well*, *glad* and possibly *ill* as well as many words that begin with *a-*: *afraid*, *asleep*, *alike*, *awake*, *abroad*. We can say

> *The boy was well/glad/abroad/afraid*, etc.

but not

> **the well/glad/abroad/afraid*, etc. *boy* . . .

The status of *ill* is not wholly clear. Can we or can we not say *the ill boy*? *Glad*, moreover, has an attributive function, but only in the 'fixed phrase' *glad tidings*. On the other side there are some words which may appear in the attributive position but not in the predicative position. Examples are *main*, *mere*, *utter*:

the main decision	but not	*The decision was main,
mere ignorance	but not	*The ignorance was mere,
utter darkness	but not	*The darkness was utter.

Note also that we can say

| the top shelf | but not | *The shelf was top, |

but both

| the top boy | and | The boy was top. |

There are some words which appear in both positions but do so with quite a different meaning. There is the old joke of the lady who wanted a painting of her late husband and the artist who replied that he did not mind waiting for him. We may also note, for a difference in meaning:

> *the right girl/The girl was right.*
> *my old friend/My friend was old.*

As we have seen, there is a similar problem with *a heavy smoker* which is not related to *The smoker was heavy* and similarly with *a hard worker*, *a poor loser*, *a bad singer*, etc. For many of these, in fact, it is quite clear that the related sentence is not of the type *The smoker was heavy* but *He smokes heavily*, i.e. that the attributive adjective is not in any way to be associated with a predicative adjective but with an adverb.

We shall have similar difficulties if we treat the so-called ordinal numerals – *first*, *second*, *last*, etc. – as adjectives. For we cannot relate

> *The Frenchman was first/second/last* with
> *the first/second/last Frenchman.*

But, perhaps, we might not treat these as adjectives at all but as determinatives along with *the*, *this*, *some*, etc.

We might, because of this, be tempted to say that only predicative functions should be used as a true test of the adjective, or at least to regard this as the basic function. In fact, in the early form of transformational grammar (see p. 172) it was thought that *the good boy* should be derived from *The boy is good*. This should have the advantage that we could deal with *the heavy smoker* in a different way by deriving it from *He smokes heavily*, the attributive function thus being derived in different ways in English. But there are further difficulties. We might say that *abroad* and *asleep* were true adjectives, though of a special kind which in attributive position followed their noun instead of preceding it, as in *people abroad*, *children asleep*. In view of the fact that most adjectives in French follow the noun this would seem quite plausible. It then might follow that *here* and *there* were also adjectives in view of:

> *The men are here/there.*
> *the men here/there.*

Equally we shall have to treat *in the garden* as an adjectival phrase in view of:

> *The children are in the garden.*
> *the children in the garden.*

In some works words such as *abroad* are treated as 'adjuncts' rather than as adjectives; semantically most of them are distinguished as place and time markers. But there are some words of this kind that may occupy the position before the noun as well as after it – *upstairs*, *inside*, etc.:

> *the upstairs room/the room upstairs*
> *the inside wall/the wall inside*

Are these adjectives in the first example but adjuncts in the second?

There are other features that may be associated with adjectives and used as criteria for establishing this class. First, they may be preceded by words like *very*. This could be said to be quite an important criterion; we can establish that *interesting* may be an adjective, while *singing* may not, by using the *very* test

> *The book is interesting/very interesting.*
> *The bird is singing/*very singing.*
> *The interesting/very interesting book.*
> *The singing/*very singing bird.*

It should also be noted that the verb, but not the adjective, may have an object as in *This book is interesting me*. We find that many verbs of a similar type, *frighten*, *shock*, *please*, etc. have related adjectival forms – *This book is frightening/shocking* and also *very frightening/shocking*. We must say, then, that with these the *-ing* form can be a true adjective – formed by derivation (p. 54). To return to our previous examples, we find we can say *The boy is very glad/well/afraid* but not . . . *very abroad* nor, except perhaps in joking form, . . . *very asleep* or *very awake*. This test does not, then, give us any clear answers. It would permit us to treat *afraid* as an adjective but to exclude *abroad*, although on the previous predicative/attributive tests these would seem to pass or fail together. It would also exclude *upstairs*, *inside*, etc., which have the maximum freedom of occurrence – before the noun, after the noun, and in the predicative position, yet would include *top* and *bottom* which are far more restricted:

> *the top shelf/the very top shelf,*

but not

The shelf was top.

Clearly, then, occurrence with *very* will not give us a clear decision whether a word is or is not an adjective.

A further possible criterion for the adjective is that it has comparative and superlative forms – *nice, nicer, nicest* and *beautiful, more beautiful, most beautiful*. It should be remembered first, however, that some of the words described as adverbs have similar forms *fast, faster, fastest* and *quickly, more quickly, most quickly*. This test will exclude most of the doubtful words – *here, there, abroad, asleep*, etc., *downstairs, inside*, etc., *top* and *bottom*, as well as *main, mere, utter* and in the attributive function *right, late* (but not *old – an older friend*). And it will permit us to treat *heavy* and *bad* as adjectives in *heavy smoker* and *bad singer*. But is this perhaps not too restrictive a criterion? We shall be left with only the 'central' class of adjectives.

The difficulties we have been discussing arise from the fact that not all words that we want to put in a single class have all the functions of that class. There is another problem that arises from what is almost the converse situation, that some words seem to belong to more than one class. Examples of this are *steel* and *cotton* in *Steel is strong, a steel bridge* and *Cotton comes from Egypt, cotton shirt*. In the first of each pair the words would seem to be nouns, in the second they seem to be adjectives. Some decades ago there was a famous argument over the question whether these were adjectives or nouns being used as adjectives. If it is accepted that they are nouns used as adjectives, we can say, conversely, that adjectives are used as nouns in the analysis of *poor* or *blue* in *the poor, the blues*.

There are many other words that seem to belong to several classes. *Love* and *work* in English seem to be both noun and verb, *safe* and *choice* to be both adjective and noun. *Round* seems to be a noun, an adjective, a verb, a preposition and an adverb – *a round of toast, a round ball, to round the Horn, round the mulberry bush* and *make it go round*! We could, if we wished, say that these belong to the rather special classes of noun-verb, adjective-noun, noun-adjective-verb-preposition-adverb. This would certainly save us listing them more than once in each class. This solution was quite seriously suggested by Hockett who recognized seven major classes – N, A, V, NA, NV, AV and NAV – plus an eighth, particles. But this is pointless. We shall never need to list all the members of each class. Rather we shall list (in the dictionary) all the words of the language and nothing at all is gained by stating that *work* belongs to the class NV rather than that it belongs to the classes N and V (N = noun, V = verb, A = adjective). There are many possible solutions to this problem, but the simplest is to treat these words in terms of derivation, but derivation involving no change of form. Since we can allow in inflectional morphology that *sheep* is both singular and plural or that *hit* is both present and past, with no overt marker of plural or past, so, too, we can say that *steel* the adjective is a derived form of *steel* the noun. Some justification for this can be found in the fact that although there is no difference of form with *steel*, *stone*, *iron*, *cotton*, there is a difference between *wood* and its derivative *wooden* or *wool* and *woollen*. Moreover, if we treat the noun *blue* as a derived form from the adjective, we can easily explain why (as a noun) it has the plural *blues*. It is not always going to be easy to decide which is the basic form and which is derived (e.g. in the case of *love* and *work*), but this is a problem that all dictionary makers have to decide, and there are usually some reasons for choosing one rather than the other as basic.

A rather different issue is raised by expressions such as *bus stop*, *shoe polish*, *bread shop*. Here we do not need to treat the first word of each of these as a derived adjective, but simply to recognize that English allows constructions that consist of two nouns. The main reason for this is that in English any noun can be placed before another noun with a kind of prepositional meaning – 'a stop for buses', 'polish for shoes'. We can extend the list of nouns so placed together almost ad infinitum *bus stop girl*, *bus stop girl inquiry*, *bus stop girl inquiry row*, etc., though these are more typical of newspaper headlines than of ordinary English. But here we do not need to talk about adjectival function, because this is a function of all nouns. This construction is clearly distinguished from the adjective–noun construction by stress. We may contrast *stéel brídge* with two stresses and *stéel company* with only one, and similarly compare the functions of *silver* in *silver box* to mean either 'box made of silver' or 'box for silver'.

Finally, let us return to the problem of distinguishing inflection and derivation, recalling that in general inflection is regular and involves morphosyntactic categories, and that derivation may involve a change of word class, whereas inflection does not. The distinction is not always clear. It might be thought that the comparative and superlative forms of adjectives (*bigger*, *biggest*) is a matter of inflection, since they do not change word class and are regular. But no morphosyntactic categories are involved, and all except the more common adjectives do not have such forms, but use *more* and *most* (*more beautiful*, *most beautiful*). It might be argued that this is more a matter of derivation. On the other hand, tense, past, present and, in some languages, future, does not seem to affect the syntax, but it is so closely bound up with person and number that it is almost always regarded as a matter of inflection.

Some extremely regular formations, however, involve a change of word class. 'Participles' and 'verbal nouns', for instance, such as *singing*, *playing* in English, or *amans*, *amaturus*, *amandum*, *amatus*, *amare* in Latin, seem to be forms of verbs, but to have the function of nouns or adjectives. Do we then say they are not inflected forms, but derived forms like *singer*? There is a rather striking situation in the Cushitic (Ethiopian) language Bilin. The genitive ('possessive') forms of the noun function like adjectives and have all the morphological features of the adjective. For instance, the word for *man* is *gerwa* and the word for *man's* is *gerwix^w* but *gerwix^w* is not only the genitive of *gerwa* but is also an adjective in the nominative case. If we want to say *to the man's mother*, not only does the word for *mother* have to be placed in the dative case, but also the word for *the man's*, since it is an adjective; the form is *gerwix^{w}əd*. In this language forms of nouns not only function like adjectives syntactically, but also regularly have the morphology of the adjective, as well as retaining the morphology of the noun! There is no problem about stating the facts in all these cases, but there is a problem in deciding whether they are matters of inflection or derivation. At a practical level they can be handled in the grammar, for they do not need to be stated individually for each word in the lexicon. But that may only prove that the distinction between inflection and derivation is not simply a distinction between grammatical and lexical morphology.

2.4 Sentence, clause and phrase

In traditional grammars 'sentence', like 'word', is a basic though
largely undefined term. Sentences are thus simply 'composed of
words', and it is the function of syntax to state what words can
be combined with others to form sentences and in what order.

Most people are quite clear in their own mind that they know
exactly what a sentence is. This confidence arises because in a
literate society we are taught to indicate sentences in our writing
by putting in the punctuation. The normal mark of the sentence
is the full stop; it would be an error of punctuation to mark the
end of a sentence with a comma. In addition new sentences must
begin with capital letters. This does not, however, help us to
understand what a sentence is. It certainly does not give us a
definition. In fact, we are taught at school to recognize sentences
through practice, not by a set of rules.

The traditional grammars, however, sometimes provide a kind
of definition: a sentence is the 'expression of a complete thought'.
But this is notional and shares all the faults of the notional
definitions that we discussed in Chapter 1. How do we know
what a complete thought is? Is 'cabbage' or 'man' a complete
thought? If not, why not? And is *If it rains, I shan't come* one
thought, or two joined together? It would seem quite impossible
to provide any definition along these lines. Equally it is impossible to provide a logical definition for the sentence. One such
would be that it contains a subject and predicate – that on the
one hand it indicates something that we are talking about, and
on the other it says something about it. For instance, in *John is
coming* we are talking about John, the subject, and also saying
that he is coming, the predicate. The difficulty here is that, if this
definition is to be of any use, we must be able to identify what
we are talking about, and very often we talk about several things
at once. For instance, in the sentence *John gave the book to
Mary* we are clearly talking about *John*, *the book* and *Mary* and
all three might seem to be the 'subject' in this sense. A natural
reaction, especially from someone who has learnt some traditional grammar, might be to say that we are talking about John
and that what we are saying about him is that he gave the book
to Mary. But this begs the question. It defines the subject as the
grammatical subject, and the grammatical subject can only be
defined in terms of the sentence. Moreover the grammatical
subject often does not indicate what we are 'talking about'. In

The birds have eaten all the fruit it is probable that what we are talking about is the missing fruit and not the unidentified birds! More strikingly, in *It's raining* what is the subject? *It*? But what is 'It'? – the weather, the universe, or what?

Even if we have learnt by some means or other at school to put our full stops and our capital letters in the right places and even if, therefore, it is possible to establish just how many sentences there are on the page, it would be a mistake to think that speech is equally made up of sentences. As we saw in Chapter 1, although sections of speech are often marked by intonation, it is not the case that every intonation tune will mark a stretch of speech that, if written, would begin with a capital letter and end with a full stop. Moreover a great deal of spoken language does not consist of sentences in the sense in which the term is understood for writing at all. Much of it is made up of incomplete, interrupted, unfinished, or even quite chaotic sentences. Speech may be made up of utterances, but utterances seldom correspond to sentences. We could not, for instance, identify all the sentences in a conversation that went:

MARY: John! Coming?
JOHN: Yes dear, I was only –
MARY: Oh do hurry up and – we ought to catch the bus – only they don't always run on time – wretched people – as long as you're quick. I've been ready for some – since half past seven.

Such a conversation is not abnormal; much of our everyday speech is like this.

A linguistic definition of the sentence must be in terms of its internal structure. A sentence will be composed of certain specified elements in a certain order, ultimately, of course, of words or parts of words. A statement then of the structures will provide us with a definition of the sentence. For instance, we might argue that the basic sentence structures of English are of the type NV, NVA, NVN, NVNN. Examples would be *John came*, *John is good*, *John saw Bill*, *John made Bill president*. (This is by no means a complete list.) All other sentences could be regarded as derived from these by either addition, e.g. of adverbs – *John came quickly* – or by expansion (see pp. 122–4): instead of *John* we could have *the boy*, *the little boy*, *the silly little boy* and even *the silly little boy on the other side of the room*. But this is not really satisfactory. We can say that a sentence is a linguistic item that has the structure we assign to the sentence. But why these structures? In particular, why not much larger structures? Why do we not want to consider *It's raining, I'm not going out* as a single sentence? The answer is that these sentence structures are the largest that can be handled in a grammatical description. We can make an accurate statement about the limitations on the co-occurrence of the items in the sentence, but we cannot with any accuracy deal with larger structures. This was put quite clearly by Bloomfield, who defined a sentence as 'an independent linguistic form, not included by virtue of any grammatical construction in any larger linguistic form'. He considered the example: *How are you? It's a fine day. Are you going to play tennis this afternoon?* and went on to show that there are no grammatical restraints linking these into a single structure; they have to be regarded as three separate units, that is to say, three sentences.

The sentence is, then, the largest unit to which we can assign a grammatical structure. Nevertheless, it would be an error to believe that outside the sentence there are no restraints, no features that link one sentence to another. There are, on the contrary, plenty. Many words such as *however, therefore, later, other* serve very often to refer from one sentence to another. More striking perhaps are what are sometimes called the 'pro-forms' of a language. Pronouns are familiar enough. *He, she* and *it* may 'stand for' *the man, the woman, the table*, etc. We find in one sentence *The man . . .* but in the next, *He . . .* But there are also 'pro-verbs'. *Did* in *John came and so did Mary* clearly stands for *came* – Mary came. All the auxiliary verbs in English can act as pro-verbs in the sense that they alone stand for the whole of the verbal element of which they are or were only the first word:

John is coming.	*Is he?*
I haven't seen him.	*But I have.*
Must you come?	*I really must.*
He'll have been there.	*No he won't.*

The verb DO is particularly important because it is the pro-form used where there is no auxiliary verb:

> *He came yesterday.   No, he didn't.*

Beyond the sentence there is no clear limit at all. In writing we use paragraphs, but what are the rules for paragraphing? There are, perhaps, some vague rules – that we start a new paragraph where we start on a new subject – but one may well suspect that paragraphs are also dictated by purely aesthetic considerations; pages without paragraphs look uninteresting. We may not, perhaps, like Alice, demand conversation or pictures in our books but we like paragraphs.

A problem is raised by the incomplete, interrupted 'sentences' that we discussed earlier (p. 67). Some linguists have argued that they should be analysed independently and treated as possible structures of the English language. But this would seem to be a mistake, above all because there would then be an infinite number of structures and no grammar could claim even partial completeness. There are, however, three kinds of 'incomplete sentence'.

First, there are those that are caused by interruptions or changes of mind on the part of the speaker. In the imaginary conversation on page 67 we find examples in *I was only* – and *I've been ready for some* – . These raise no problems for grammar; they are genuinely incomplete sentences, understandable and analysable as such. (The linguist may not be altogether uninterested in them, however; he may well want to know whether there are conditions for interrupting, for hesitation, change of mind, etc.)

Secondly, there are incomplete sentences that are dependent on what has gone before. *John*, for instance, might be a reply to *Who did it?* or *Who did you see?* It can therefore be reasonably understood as an incomplete form of *John did it* or *I saw John*. These make extensive use of pro-forms and are to be analysed in terms of the complete, expanded, 'original' form. They are 'contextually' conditioned and can only be understood as such.

Thirdly, there are incomplete sentences such as *Coming? Coming! Found them? Got you!* which might seem equally to be shortened forms of *Are you coming? I'm coming! Have you found them? I've got you!* But these are not contextually conditioned; they do not in any way depend on what has gone before. There is a case for treating them as English sentences in their own right, but there is also an argument for treating them as derived from the longer forms by 'deletion' – we 'delete' the pronoun and the auxiliary verb.

The sentence consists of words, but the words are grouped into elements that are smaller than the sentence. For these most linguists use the term 'phrase'. Sentences are thus analysable into phrases. The most important phrases of the sentences are the verb phrases and the noun phrases (symbolized as VP and NP respectively), e.g.

> *John   likes   Mary*   (NP   VP   NP).

(However, the term VP is used in a rather different sense in the phrase structure analysis of transformational generative grammar – see 4.2.) A phrase in this sense can be a single word, but the phrases are often much longer than single words:

> *The little boy   has been reading   a fairy story*   (NP   VP   NP).

In addition there are elements within the sentence such as *this morning* or *in the garden* which are sometimes called 'adjuncts' but are better called 'adverbial' phrases.

The structure of the noun phrase and the verb phrase will vary from language to language. If we consider the simplest phrases (but see below, pp. 142–3) of English, we find that a noun phrase consists either of a pronoun alone (or, rarely, with an adjective, e.g. *Poor you!*), or of a noun preceded by various words some of which are adjectives and other determinatives (*the, this, my,* etc.), and sometimes followed by a word such as *abroad* or *asleep* (*people abroad, children asleep*). In fact the modifiers of the noun phrase, all the words that is to say except the noun itself, are of numerous and varied types. In particular they have their own place in the sequence. Not only can we not place *asleep* before the noun (**asleep children*), but we have to put the adjectives in the right order (*little red hen,* not **red little hen*) putting also any other elements before or after the adjectives and in their right order. This is clearly shown by the following sequences which permit little or no variation:

> *All the twenty-five little English children.*
> *Both her worn-out red cotton dresses.*

The study of the noun phrase itself is worthy of a complete book.

So too is the verb phrase. Its structure is a little less complex in some ways, somewhat more complex in others. The maximum length of a verb phrase seems to be five words, e.g.:

> *He may have been being beaten,*

though it may be doubted whether all five often occur together. There are certainly five elements that occur in sequence:

(1) a modal followed by the simple form of a verb.
(2) HAVE followed by the past participle (the perfect).
(3) BE followed by the *-ing* form of the verb (the 'progressive' or 'continuous').
(4) BE followed by the past participle (the passive).
(5) the main verb.

It is in this context, the analysis of sentences into NPs and VPs, that we can talk of 'subjects' and 'objects'. Instead of treating *John likes Mary* as NP–VP–NP, we can describe it as subject–verb–object, and say that *John* is the subject and *Mary* the object of the verb *likes*. It is, however, a little misleading to use the term 'verb' at this level, and so to analyse *John likes Mary* as subject–verb–object. For the term 'verb' is used as the name of the word class, like 'noun'. Strictly, we need another term for the sentence element, and PREDICATOR has been suggested. The sentence can either be treated as N–V–N (or, more strictly, as NP–VP–NP) or as subject–predicator–object. Unfortunately, the term 'verb' is regularly used in this other sense, and this practice will be followed with reluctance; but it should be remembered that 'verb' is ambiguous, referring either to the word class or the sentence element. We shall return to subjects and objects later (pp. 75–7).

One further traditional distinction is between TRANSITIVE and INTRANSITIVE sentences, transitive sentences being those with objects (*John likes Mary*) and intransitive those without (*John sings*) (and we may similarly refer to the transitive and intransitive verbs LOVE and SING). This distinction is related to voice (p. 88), since only transitive verbs in English may have passives. We may also, perhaps, talk of di-transitive verbs, those that have two objects (*John gave Mary a present*); here *Mary* is described as the INDIRECT object and *a present* as the DIRECT object. In some languages even further distinctions can be made (p. 76). But there are, in English and most other languages, many other sentence types for which no similar names are available (see p. 74).

Traditional grammars also talk of 'clauses', which are 'sentences that are part of larger sentences'. This definition is, strictly, self-contradictory, but it still indicates what is meant, and illustrates a very important characteristic of natural

languages. In, for instance, *John stood still and Mary ran away*
we have a 'larger-sentence' consisting of two sentences joined
together by *and*. Similarly in *While John was standing there Mary
ran away* there are two sentences, the first introduced by *while*,
making up the larger sentence.

However, these two larger sentences illustrate two different
ways in which sentences may be joined together. In the first,
they are simply linked by *and*, and we can link as many as we
wish in this way. Moreover, the relationship between the two
sentences is not very different from that of two sentences
separated by a full stop. There would be little difference in, for
instance, *John stood still. Mary ran away*. (It is not true, however,
that we can link any two sentences with *and*. We cannot say
Come here and John has arrived though we can say *Come here.
John has arrived*. But, for the most part, there are few restrictions
on sentences joined by *and*.) This kind of linking of sentences is
known as 'coordination'.

The second way in which two sentences may form a larger
sentence is one in which, instead of the two sentences being
joined together as equals, one of the sentences functions as part
of the other. For instance, alongside *He said many things*, we
can say *He said that he was coming*. Clearly *that he was coming*
has the same kind of function as *many things*, and is, perhaps,
the object of *He said* ... A term used for this today is
'embedding', one sentence being embedded within another. The
traditional grammars referred to this as 'subordination' and
talked about the embedded sentence as a 'subordinate clause'.
These subordinate clauses were further classified into noun-
clauses, adjective-clauses and adverb-clauses, according to
whether they had the function of nouns, adjectives or adverbs
within the other sentence (the 'main' clause). For instance, in
the example we have just mentioned *that he was coming* has the
function of a noun, for it is nouns and noun phrases that act as
objects. An example of an adjective clause would be *who was
standing there* in *The boy who was standing there ran away*. It has
a function similar to that of *little* in *the little boy*, though the rules
of English permit *little* to come before *boy* but the adjective
clause to come after it. An adverb clause would be *while I was
standing there*, which has the same kind of function as *yesterday*
in *I saw John while I was standing there*.

The traditional grammars reserve the term sentence for the

larger or 'maximal' sentence and talk about the sentences of which it is composed, the 'minimal' sentences, as clauses. This is an important distinction, since there are features of the clause that are not features of the larger sentence. Reflexive pronouns, for instance (p. 59), will normally refer to a noun within the same clause (but not to one in another clause in the same sentence), as shown by

> *The boy said that John had hurt himself.*

Here *himself* can refer only to *John*, not to *the boy*.

The grammars make a distinction, moreover, between 'clause' and 'phrase', though not using 'phrase' in the sense in which I have used it (to distinguish the essential parts of a sentence – the noun phrase, the verb phrase, etc.), but to refer (amongst other things) to a special kind of embedded sentence – one without a finite verb. A 'finite verb' is a verb form that can stand alone in an independent sentence – *comes* is finite but *coming* is not, since we can say *He comes every day* but not **He coming every day*. We are told therefore that *how to do this* in *I don't know how to do this* is a noun phrase, not a noun clause, because it has no finite verb. But this seems an unimportant distinction. There are all sorts of rules for embedding or subordination, but what is important is that the embedded sentence has still many of the characteristics of a sentence. In the example above we still have a predicator *do* and object *this*. In *I don't like John doing that* we have *John* (subject) *doing* (predicator) and *that* (object) – an almost normal sentence, but without a finite form of a verb. We shall discuss some of these problems again later.

In this chapter we have talked about 'analysing' sentences. Traditional grammar made analysis or 'parsing', as it was often called, an essential exercise. In Nesfield, for instance, we are instructed to divide a sentence first into subject and predicate, then to divide the subject into nominative and its enlargement and finally its predicate into finite verb, completion and extension, the completion being either object or complement or both. For the sentences *The new master soon put the class into good order* and *A bird in the hand is worth two in the bush* the analysis is:

1. Subject		2. Predicate			
Nominative or Equivalent	*Enlargement*	*Finite verb*	Completion		*Extension*
			Object	*Complement*	
master	(1) The (2) new	put	the class	into good order	soon
bird	(1) A (2) in the hand	is	—	worth two in the bush	—

This indicates in some degree the structure of the sentence, but is, even within its own lights, far from satisfactory. Why, for instance, do we have enlargement only for the nominative? The enlargement includes all of what today would be called the modifier of the noun – the article and the adjective, etc. But all nouns in the sentence may have similar modifiers too. *The* occurs as a modifier in *the class* which is the object, and in *the bush* which is part of the complement, and nouns can equally occur in the extension as part of prepositional phrases. It is misleading too to talk about 'completions' which are required, according to Nesfield, because some verbs 'do not make sense in themselves' but need either objects (the transitive verbs) or complements (the copulative verbs). For there are verbs which seem also to require extensions. An example is *to lie* (as in *to lie down*) which needs such extensions as *there* or *on the table* (*it lay there/on the table*). In fact, if we investigate carefully we shall find that verbs can be classified into a number of different types, each requiring a different set of following grammatical elements. We need to recognize at least seven sentence structures, exemplified by:

(1) *The man smiled*. (NV)
(2) *John seems happy*. (NVA)
(3) *The woman hit the man*. (NVN)
(4) *I gave the boy a book*. (NVNN)
(5) *The boy sat on the floor*. (NVPN)
(6) *The girl made John happy*. (NVAN)

(7) *John put the book on the table*. (NVNPN)

Also, it would usually be said that, in spite of their superficial similarity to (3) and (4), different analyses are required for:

(8) *The woman became a teacher*.
(9) *I made the boy their leader*.

For (8), part of the argument would be that there is no passive, as there is for (3) (*The man was hit by the woman* but not **A teacher was become by the woman*), and for (9) that we cannot say **I made their leader to the boy*, by analogy with *I gave a book to the boy*. Such arguments take us further than the immediately observable structures.

Let us now return briefly to subjects and objects. It is clear that these are not merely elements or constituents of sentences, as NPs and VPs are, but that they are essentially functional or relational (and they have been described as 'grammatical relations').

We can and must define subjects and objects formally. In English the relevant criteria are position in the sentence, agreement of the subject with the verb and morphology in the case of pronouns (*I* vs. *me*, etc.). There is some temptation also to define the subject as the 'actor', the person who performs the action, and the object the 'goal' or 'recipient', the person or thing that is affected by it. But this would not allow us to identify the subject as *John* in any of the following sentences, for in none of them is *John* 'acting' in any intelligible sense:

> *John suffered terribly.*
> *John looked sad.*
> *John saw his brother.*
> *John sank under the waves.*

It would be equally impossible to determine the subject in

> *John lent a book to Bill.*

in view of

> *Bill borrowed a book from John.*

Who is the actor, who the recipient? If *John* is the subject in the first sentence, *Bill* cannot be the subject in the second as long as we rely on purely notional definitions. But there is no real doubt in linguistic terms – in terms of position in the sentence. Nevertheless, although we cannot define subjects in terms of being agents, we can say that subjects are typically agents, just as plural typically refers to more than one (p. 35). That is to say, where we can establish subjects on formal grammatical grounds, we shall find considerable, but not absolute, correlation with the notion of agency.

Naturally, not all languages mark subjects and objects in the same way. In Latin, for instance (see the example on p. 20), word order is not a defining characteristic, while case-marking is. In other languages, e.g. Swahili, the main criterion is agreement of both subject and object with the verb. Nor are subject and object the only grammatical relations. In English we need to distinguish direct objects and indirect objects (see p. 71), while in other languages instruments and beneficiaries are clearly marked formally.

More surprisingly, perhaps, it is by no means certain that the relations of subject and object are appropriate for the description of all languages. There are probably few languages, if any, that do not have some means of indicating actors and goals. Yet it has been reported that there is at least one (Lisu, Lolo-Burmese) that does not mark this distinction in any regular formal way, so that a single sentence may mean either 'People bite dogs' or 'Dogs bite people'. This seldom creates any ambiguity, however, since either the context or common sense will usually point to the correct meaning; where ambiguity is likely, it is always possible to add some extra comment.

More important are the languages with ERGATIVE systems. These differ from our familiar subject–object system in a fundamental way. The need to distinguish subjects and objects arises only where there are two NPs in a sentence; there is no need for the distinction where there is only one NP – in an intransitive sentence. Yet English and other familiar languages always mark this single NP in the same way as the subject of the transitive sentence. In an ergative system the single NP is identified with the other NP of the transitive sentence – the one we should call the 'object'. It is rather as if English said *Him sings instead of He sings. An example from Dyirbal (Australia) is:

ŋuma banaganyu.	'Father returned'.
yabu banaganyu.	'Mother returned'.
ŋuma yabuŋgu buṛan.	'Mother saw father'.
yabu ŋumaŋgu buṛan.	'Father saw mother'.

Notice that in the third and fourth sentences it is the words for 'father' and 'mother' respectively that have no endings (as in the first and second), while the ending -ŋgu appears on 'mother' and 'father'. If we continue to use the terms 'subject' and 'object' here there are grave problems. We could say that intransitive sentences have only objects and no subjects. Alternatively, we might simply say that the subjects of intransitive sentences are marked in the same way as the objects of transitive ones. But this would be paradoxical and difficult to explain; it would be to impose our own familiar system upon an unfamiliar one, just as Latin grammar was imposed upon all kinds of languages. Instead, it is usual now to refer to the NP of the intransitive sentence together with the 'object' of the transitive as ABSOLUTIVE, and to the other NP of the transitive, its 'subject', as ERGATIVE. Reference was made earlier to 'ergative systems', not, as is usual, to 'ergative languages', because, curiously, the languages never seem to use the ergative system throughout all their syntax. Nevertheless, languages with ergative systems are found all over the world and should neither be ignored nor forced into the subject–object mould. They include Basque, Eskimo, Caucasian languages such as Georgian, North Indian languages such as Hindi and Bengali, and many languages in Australia.

2.5 Grammatical categories

We mentioned in Chapter 1 the grammatical categories of number, gender and tense. These and others are an essential part of traditional grammar, especially the grammar of the classical languages, though to a varying degree they are also used in the description of modern languages. Some, e.g. gender, are regarded as categories of the noun – nouns are either masculine or feminine (or neuter); others, e.g. tense, are regarded as categories of the verb – past, present, or future; while others, e.g. number, seem to belong to both – in *The boys are* both *boys* and *are* are plural.

There are two respects in which the traditional grammars can be criticized. First, as we have seen, they often define the categories in 'notional' terms. Plural is defined as 'more than one', gender is identified with sex, or tense with time. In spite of this the grammars often produce the same results as an analysis in formal terms; they do not, for instance, fail to recognize *oats* as plural and *wheat* as singular. Secondly, and this too was briefly mentioned, they often take over the categories of Latin and impose them upon English or whatever language they are describing.

In this section I propose to look briefly with examples at some of these grammatical categories. Most of them will be familiar, but others less so, and as we look at less familiar languages we shall find that they have to be interpreted in rather surprising ways. But before proceeding it would be useful to list some of the traditional categories with an indication of the term used, the class of word with which it is generally found and the kind of meaning with which it is (sometimes misleadingly) associated.

GENDER masculine, feminine (and commonly neuter) – a feature of nouns, associated with male, female and (for neuter) sexless creatures – but often misleadingly so.

NUMBER singular, plural (and sometimes dual) – a feature of nouns and verbs, associated with 'one' and 'more than one' (dual with 'two').

PERSON first person, second person, third person – a classification of the pronouns and a feature of verbs – *I, we*; *you*; *he, she, it, they*.

TENSE present, past, future – a feature of verbs, associated with time.

MOOD indicative, subjunctive and, in classical Greek, optative – a feature of the verb, associated with statements of fact versus possibility, supposition, etc.

VOICE active and passive – again a feature of verbs – the object of the active becoming the subject of the passive.

CASE nominative, vocative, accusative, genitive, dative and ablative – a feature of the noun, associated with a variety of largely unrelated semantic and grammatical features, but illustrated by the translations *boy* (subject), *O boy, boy* (object), *of a boy, to* or *for a boy, from* or *by a boy*.

These are mostly morphosyntactic categories, and all can be defined formally.

Let us consider GENDER. We have already seen examples of French and German – *le livre* (masculine) 'the book', *la porte* (feminine) 'the door'; *der Tisch* (masculine) 'the table', *die Tür* (feminine) 'the door', *das Feuer* (neuter) 'the fire'. In these and other European languages gender may be defined in terms of the form of the article and adjectives that may accompany the noun.

Articles and adjectives are said to 'agree' with nouns. Examples from Spanish are (note that the adjective comes last):

> *el libro rojo* (masculine)   'the red book'
> *la puerta roja* (feminine)   'the red door'

Here we have the contrast of *el* and *la* and of the endings *-o* and *-a* and these are determined by the noun, *libro* requiring one of each pair, *puerta* the other. Russian has no articles, but the adjectives agree:

> *novyj stul* (masculine)   'new chair'
> *novaja kniga* (feminine)   'new book'
> *novoe okno* (neuter)   'new window'

The point that gender is defined in these languages in terms of the agreement of the adjective and (in some languages) of the article cannot be over-emphasized. Yet in some languages it is possible to recognize the gender of a word by the shape of the word itself. Thus in both Spanish and Italian words ending in *-o* are usually masculine, and words ending in *-a* are feminine. But there are many exceptions – *el poema*, *il poema* 'the poem', *la mano*, *la mano* 'the hand' (Spanish example first, Italian second). Similarly in Latin the nouns of the first declension all end in *-a* in the nominative and are mostly feminine, while the nouns of the second declension all end in *-us* or *-um* and are mainly masculine and neuter respectively. But again we cannot define first declension nouns as feminine and second declension nouns as masculine or neuter according to their endings because *agricola* 'a farmer' (first declension) is masculine, hence we have *agricola bonus* 'a good farmer' not **agricola bona*, while *fagus* 'beech' (second declension) is feminine, and there are many other examples. By contrast, all nouns ending in *-um* are neuter.

In European languages gender does not usually affect the verb – it is only the adjectives and articles that agree with the noun. In Russian, however, there are distinct past tense forms of the verb for masculine and feminine (in the singular):

> *on pisal*   'he wrote'
> *ona pisala*   'she wrote'

In many Semitic languages, gender (along with person and number) is regularly marked in the verb. In Geez (Classical Ethiopic), for instance, the paradigm of the verb reads:

nagara	'he spoke'
nagarat	'she spoke'
nagarka	'you (a man) spoke'
nagarki	'you (a woman) spoke'
nagarku	'I spoke'
nagaru	'they (men) spoke'
nagara	'they (women) spoke'
nagarkem	'you (men) spoke'
nagarken	'you (women) spoke'
nagarna	'we spoke'

If we think about the definition of gender in terms of classes of noun with which adjectives and possibly verbs agree, and pay no attention to the non-grammatical feature of sex, gender is found in many other languages in a surprising form. In Swahili, for instance, there are word classes which differ in not only having different prefixes but also in requiring similar differences in the adjectives and the verbs. Thus we find:

mtu mzuri	'a fine man'
nyumba nzuri	'a fine house'
kitu kizuri	'a fine thing'
kasha zuri	'a fine chest'
mahali pazuri	'a fine place'
kufa kuzuri	'a fine death'

In these it will be seen that the word meaning 'fine' (*zuri*) is preceded by *m-*, *n-*, *ki-*, nothing, *pa-* and *ku-* according to the noun with which it agrees. There are, in fact, two other classes which I have not given because in the singular they require the same prefix as the first class (*m-*), but each class of these has a different plural form so that we get also (to take the first class and only one of the other classes):

mtu mzuri	'a fine man'
watu wazuri	'fine men'
mti mzuri	'a fine tree'
miti mizuri	'fine trees'

But not only adjectives agree with the nouns; so also do verbs, as in:

Mtu mzuri amekuja   'The fine man has come.'

but

Kitu kizuri kimevunjika   'The fine thing is broken.'

Here the *m-* class nouns require a verb form with an initial *a-* while the *ki-* class nouns require an initial *ki-*.

There is no reference to sex in Swahili gender. In fact there is no consistently clear difference of meaning between the various classes, except that the first class refers exclusively to living creatures, to 'animates', while the third class (with *ki-*) refers mostly to small things and the fourth mostly to large things. There are similar classes in some American Indian languages and in these the meanings are rather more surprising. In, for instance, the Algonquian languages there are two noun classes distinguished in terms of agreement of the verb. These two classes are referred to as 'animate' and 'inanimate' since the former includes all the words for persons and animals and the latter most other words. But the words for 'raspberry', 'kettle' and 'knee' belong to the animate class, though the words for 'strawberry', 'bowl' and 'elbow' belong to the inanimate class. This classification is one of gender, if gender is defined in terms of agreement. It is precisely because there is no one-to-one correlation between the form and the meaning that we are justified in doing this. We have already seen that in European languages gender does not equal sex. There is equally no difficulty about using the terms 'animate' and 'inanimate' even if 'animate' includes objects that are not alive. The labels are chosen because they indicate typical, but not defining, semantic characteristics of the class. (Linguistics is not the only discipline that uses such an approach. The giant panda lives exclusively on bamboo shoots, but is classified zoologically as a carnivore.)

NUMBER raises fewer problems. The European languages have the distinction of singular and plural, marked in both the noun and the verb, the verb usually agreeing with the subject. In English this is almost extinct but still to be found in *The boy comes*, *The boys come*. In other European languages there is agreement with article and adjectives as well as the verb – French *le petit garçon*, *les petits garçons*, Italian *il ragazzo piccolo*, *i ragazzi piccoli* 'the little boy', 'the little boys'. Some languages have singular, dual (two) and plural. Classical Greek was one, and Classical Arabic. Thus in Arabic we find *malikun* 'a king', *malikāni* 'two kings', *malikūna* 'kings', and if we look to the verb there are no less than thirteen forms in the paradigm (for gender is marked too):

3 m.s.	*kataba*	'he wrote'
3 f.s.	*katabat*	'she wrote'
2 m.s.	*katabta*	'you (a man) wrote'
2 f.s.	*katabti*	'you (a woman) wrote'
1 m/f.s.	*katabtu*	'I wrote'
3 m.du.	*katabā*	'they (two men) wrote'
3 f.du.	*katabatā*	'they (two women) wrote'
2 m/f.du.	*katabtumā*	'you (two) wrote'
3 m.pl.	*katabū*	'they (men) wrote'
3 f.pl.	*katabna*	'they (women) wrote'
2 m.pl.	*katabtum*	'you (men) wrote'
2 f.pl.	*katabtunna*	'you (women) wrote'
1 m/f.pl.	*katabnā*	'we wrote'

But even this is simple compared with some languages. In Fijian the system of pronouns makes the distinction between singular, dual, 'little plural' and 'big plural'. In Tigre too we find three forms of the noun e.g.:

färäs	'a horse'
'äfras	'horses'
'äfresam	'a few horses'

But this is not strictly the grammatical category of number, as Tigre has many other forms too – not only 'little plurals' but even 'pejorative plurals' and 'diminutives', e.g. *gäzirät* 'an island' but *gäzeram* 'some poor islands', *gäzirätit* 'a little island'. These forms do not differ in terms of number concord; most of them are singular, plural concord being restricted almost entirely to plural forms of animate nouns. Concord in terms of gender, however, is more relevant; oddly enough, *gäzeram* is masculine and *gäzirätit* is feminine. We must perhaps treat these forms within derivation rather than inflection and consider them to be on the 'edge' of grammar, not involved directly in a grammatical category of the morphosyntactic kind.

PERSON is probably the one linguistic category that has clearly defined reference to non-linguistic entities. In traditional terms first person refers to the person speaking, second person to the person spoken to, and third person to the person (or thing) spoken about. Like gender and number, person often involves features of concord, especially with the verb, and in many languages, e.g. the Semitic languages, all three categories are involved in the paradigms of the verb, as we have seen already (p. 80). In languages with little or no inflection, however, we can recognize the category of person in terms of the pronoun, the words for *I*, *you*, *he*, etc. alone. Indeed, provided we take pronouns into account, it is almost certainly a universal feature.

The definitions work well enough in the singular – a speaker, someone spoken to, someone spoken of. But in the plural it is more complex. Strictly, one might suppose, first person plural (*we*) ought to refer to a plurality of speakers, second person plural (*you*) to a plurality of people addressed and third person plural (*they*) to a plurality of people spoken of. But this is not so. The use of *we* to refer to a number of joint speakers is rare and is confined to 'choruses'. Choruses, in this sense, are not restricted to musical works or to drama (e.g. Greek comedies and tragedies); there are other kinds of chorus, e.g. the football crowd that yells 'We want four' after the third goal has been scored. Similarly, *you* does not refer only to people spoken to; it often refers to the person or persons spoken to plus others. *They* alone is restricted to our 'ideal' use; it refers solely to people spoken about. In terms of the singular pronouns the possibilities of interpretation for *we*, *you* and *they* are (with the dots to indicate that there is no upper limit of the possible numbers of 'I', 'you' or 'he' and that gender is being ignored):

we	'I and I (and I . . .)'
	'I (and I . . .) and you (and you . . .)'
	'I (and I . . .) and he (and he . . .)'
you	'you and you (and you . . .)'
	'you (and you...) and he (and he . . .)'
they	'he and he (and he . . .)'

Another, and perhaps simpler, way of stating this is to say that *we* means any group of people that includes the speaker, *you* any group that includes the person spoken to, except a group covered by *we*, and *they* any group not covered by *we* or *you*. Some languages make distinctions not found in English. A common one is between an 'exclusive' and an 'inclusive' *we*, the first standing for *I and he* (*they*) and the second for *you and I*. In Neo-Melanesian, for instance, there are pidgin forms derived from English *me-fellow* and *you-me*.

There is a still more striking complexity: person (or person together with number) is often used in what seems to be a quite inconsistent way. For instance, although we can establish a second person singular form in a language it often turns out that the form is used only for a very restricted category of persons spoken to. If we consider English *thou* and *thee*, for instance, we find that apart from the use of these forms in dialects, they are used only to address God! He is the only 'person spoken to' for whom they are appropriate. In French and Italian similar forms are used only for addressing friends, equals and close relatives. In France *tutoyer*, to use *tu* and *te*, 'means to address familiarly'. In Italy a student addressing another student would be expected to use *tu* and *te*, but not if addressing his professor! But what are the alternatives? There seem to be two common ones. One is to use the plural form, which is what English and French have done – English *you*, French *vous* – though in English the *thou*, *thee* forms are so rare that it is almost certainly best to say that today *you* is both singular and plural. Another is to use the third person instead of the second plural, as Italian has done with *Lei* and *Loro* (*Lei*, moreover, is feminine – 'literally' *she*), though the distinction is made in the writing by using capital letters for the 'second person' use. German combines both conventions. It uses the third person plural form of the pronoun instead of both the singular and the plural second person polite forms, though again using a capital initial (*Sie* as in *Sprechen Sie Deutsch?* 'Do you speak German?'). What often happens, as has happened in English, is that the distinction between second person singular and plural eventually becomes completely lost. Not surprisingly, there are dialects of English where it has been recreated, e.g. in the south of the United States, where *y'all* (*you all*) is the plural form, *you* being restricted to the singular.

There are other eccentric usages: the royal or editorial *we*, and the matronly *we* of *How are we this morning?* *You* is very common as the indefinite unspecified pronoun, though it used to be frowned upon in school and schoolchildren were recommended to use *one* instead. As we saw earlier (p. 22) *they* is often used for singular reference where sex is unspecified, e.g. *If anyone comes, they can't get in*.

The pronoun system of some languages, especially of Southeast Asia, is much more complex, since whole sets of different forms are used according to the relative rank of the speakers and people spoken to. There are what are called 'honorifics', which are sometimes reflected in mock translation of, for instance, Japanese by the use of the word *Honourable*. This system is still within the grammatical category of person though its reference includes much more than the simple distinction of person(s) speaking, person(s) spoken to and person(s) spoken about.

With TENSE we move to consider a category associated directly with the verb. We have seen already that tense is often, though very misleadingly, associated with time, and the problem of tense in English is dealt with in some detail in Appendix C. There are few, if any, languages in which there is a category that is totally related to time, though there are some, e.g. Latin, where a division into present, past and future is justified on formal grounds with some fairly clear relationship to time, e.g. *amo* 'I love', *amabo* 'I shall love', *amabam* 'I loved'; but even here *amabam* is perhaps better translated as 'I was loving' with *amavi* as the 'I loved' form. There is also the further complication that Latin has a set of 'perfect' forms with the same three tenses, *amavi* 'I have loved', *amavero* 'I shall have loved' and *amaveram* 'I had loved', and we must note that *amavi* occurs here too! Clearly Latin is a fairly complex language. Once we look at other languages many other non-correspondences between tense and time come to light. In Bilin (Ethiopian Cushitic) there are many different paradigms of the verb, translated not only by e.g. 'I see', 'I saw', 'I shall see', etc., but also 'if I see', 'that I saw', 'who sees', etc. These fall very clearly into two main groups on formal grounds – the tonal features and certain vowel qualities involving vowel harmony (see p. 45). These two groups are easily characterized as 'past' and 'present' tenses respectively, so that we find pairs differing only in tense (with these very clear features of tone and vowel quality) that would translate 'that I saw' and 'that I see' or '(I) who saw' and '(I) who see' as well as 'I saw' and 'I see'. But we then find two quite remarkable divergences between tense and time. Surprisingly all those that translate any kind of future 'I shall see', 'I should see', etc., are, in terms of the formal features, past tense. More disquieting, perhaps, the 'verb *to be*' is formed from two different verbs, one providing all the past tense forms, the other all the present tense forms; but the one that provides all the present tenses has the meaning associated with past tense and the one that provides the past tenses has the meaning associated with present tense!

For this one verb (or strictly two verbs) the usual pattern of form and meaning is totally reversed. To put the situation paradoxically, the present tenses are all past and the past tenses are all present.

In many languages there is ASPECT as well as, or instead of, tense, tense supposedly referring to time and aspect to completion, duration and similar concepts. In Latin, we can treat the distinction between the perfect tenses and the others as one of aspect. In the Slavonic languages a regular distinction is made between verbs referring to completed and those denoting non-completed action; Russian has to distinguish between reading a book but not finishing it (*čitat'*) and reading a book and finishing it (*pročitat'*). In Classical Arabic the only distinction in the verb seems to be one of aspect, complete and incomplete.

Morphologically, English has only two tenses, past and present, as illustrated by *take(s)* and *took* or *love(s)* and *loved*. The traditional 'future' tense is formed with the auxiliary verbs WILL and SHALL (see below and Appendix C). But English also has progressive (or 'continuous') forms expressed by the auxiliary verb BE followed by an -*ing* form as in:

The boy is reading a book.

It also has perfect forms which are expressed by the auxiliary HAVE and a following past participle:

The boy has read the book.

The term 'aspect' is often used to refer both to the progressive and to the perfect, though the term 'phase' has been suggested for the latter. In any case, it is important to realize that these are only labels. It is unwise to attempt to find clear semantic distinctions between aspect and tense (and phase), except where a language, such as English, has more than one such category. In other languages it is by no means clear always whether 'aspect' or 'tense' is the more appropriate label for a formal category of the verb.

Even less clearly definable in semantic terms is MOOD. In Latin and the Romance languages there is the subjunctive mood as well as the indicative (and the imperative), while Greek has the optative as well. In so far as the distinction of mood merely marks another dimension for the classification in formal terms of the verb forms, it is entirely satisfactory. In Latin we can classify them in three ways independently, in terms of tense, aspect and mood:

NON-PERFECT	INDICATIVE	SUBJUNCTIVE
present	*amo*	*amem*
future	*amabo*	—
past	*amabam*	*amarem*

PERFECT		
present	*amavi*	*amaverim*
future	*amavero*	—
past	*amaveram*	*amavissem*

(The grammar books, however, usually fail to make the non-perfect/perfect distinction so explicit in their exposition.)

The most common function of mood in Latin and Greek and other languages is its use in subordinate clauses. In Latin, for instance, the subjunctive is used for 'indirect commands', for purpose ('in order to . . .'), for clauses within reported speech, etc., while in Spanish there is a very complex system using subjunctives for the conditional clauses (those with 'if . . .'). In these, mood cannot be said to have any meaning; its use is determined quite automatically. Yet the Greek subjunctive was used in Homer for simple future time reference and the optative for vague possibility. English has no mood in this sense (but see p. 200), but it has the modals WILL, SHALL, CAN, MAY, MUST, OUGHT, and marginally DARE and NEED (p. 58). The modals can be defined formally, but share, to some degree, meanings of possibility and necessity, which justifies the use of the term. It may, moreover, be no coincidence that, just as the Greek subjunctive may refer to future time, so the traditional 'future tense' of English is formed with the modals WILL and SHALL. We may speculate that the future is seen as more potential than actual.

To look for some 'real', universal, distinction between mood and tense, or mood, aspect and tense, is almost certainly pointless. We shall find that their meanings refer to time, to possibility, to completion, etc., but seldom will there be any one-to-one relation between such meanings and the formal categories. We should be particularly careful not to take the formal categories of Latin, assign them generalized meanings and then impose them, mainly on the basis of those meanings, upon other languages.

Finally, VOICE raises a few interesting problems. Many languages show a difference between active and passive with the object of the active being the subject of the passive in such pairs of sentences as *John saw Bill* and *Bill was seen by John*. This raises some important theoretical problems that we shall discuss later, because, unlike tense and mood, voice involves a change in the position and the function of other words in the sentence.

We often find more than the two distinctions of active and passive. Greek had a third, the middle, whose meaning was generally that of doing something for oneself or to oneself. A more complex, but wholly neat, pattern is found in the Semitic languages. Consider, for instance, these forms of Tigrinya:

active	*qätäle*	'he killed'
passive	*täqätle*	'he was killed'
causative	*'aqtäle*	'he caused to kill'

A different pattern is found in Malagasy (Madagascar), which in addition to active and passive has a 'circumstantial' voice. This allows both indirect objects and instruments to become subjects. There are active and passive sentences that may be translated as:

> 'The woman bought the rice for the children with the money.'
> 'The rice was bought for the children by the woman.'

There are also two possible sentences with the circumstantial voice:

> 'The children were bought the rice by the woman.'
> 'The money was bought-with (used for buying) the rice for the children.'

Even in English it is not only the object of the active sentence that may become the subject of the passive. An indirect object or a 'prepositional' object may also be involved:

> *The boy was given a book.*
> *This bed has not been slept in.*

Moreover, why do we say *The bells rang* and *The fabric washes easily*. For we also have active sentences with *the bells* and *the fabric* as the objects – *They rang the bells* and *She washed the fabric*. It would seem that in the first two sentences *rang* and *washes* are somehow passive in meaning, though still active in form. We could, perhaps, treat them as another voice in English, perhaps the English 'middle'; but that would be misleading because there is no distinct set of forms.

I have left CASE until last because it is not a category in the same sense as the others. What we have in certain languages (Latin is a good example) is a set of forms of the noun, such as that for *amicus*, which is already given on pp. 16–17. But this is a collection of forms that are not (necessarily) similar in function. The nominative and the accusative are markers of sentence function, of subject and object respectively; this is largely true too of the dative, which marks the indirect object. In contrast, the vocative has no function at all within the sentence, but it is the form used for addressing or calling, while the main function of the genitive is within the noun phrase, to indicate the possessor, as in *pueri liber* 'the boy's book'. The ablative is mainly used after prepositions such as *ex* and *ab* with a meaning of 'from'. But to complicate matters the accusative is also used with prepositions meaning 'to'. We can do no more, then, than set out the paradigm, i.e. list forms of the noun which have a whole variety of functions. Not surprisingly, in other languages there are cases with other names and other meanings, e.g. the allative for motion towards and the comitative to translate 'with', and we have already mentioned the ergative. Finnish is often quoted as the language with the most cases – nominative (subject), genitive ('of'), accusative (object), inessive ('in'), elative ('out of'), illative ('into'), adessive ('on'), ablative ('from'), allative ('to'), essive ('as'), partitive ('involving part of'), translative ('involving change to'), abessive ('without'), instructive ('by') and comitative ('with'). But although this is interesting, it is probably misleading. For most of these 'case forms' are no more than noun forms with 'post-positions', i.e. suffixes functioning like prepositions but occurring at the end of the word instead of preceding it.

English has very little in the way of case. We can, if we wish, talk about the possessive *'s* as the genitive in e.g. *John's*, or distinguish the pronouns *I/me, he/him*, etc., in terms of case, though not in terms of the Latin nominative and accusative, since they appear not only as objects but after all prepositions and even as 'subjects' in e.g. *Who's there? Me.* But there are two words of warning. First, we must not then import case into the nouns and say that *John* and *Bill* are in different cases in *John hit Bill*. Secondly, we must not look for yet another case for *me* in *He gave me a book*. This is not dative, for English has no dative, unless we simply impose the Latin case system upon English. But why that of Latin, why not that of Finnish, Basque or Chinese?

There is, however, one interesting suggestion. If we reconsider the sentence that we discussed in the section dealing with voice: *The fabric washes well*, we can compare this not only with *She washes the fabric*, but also with *Brand X washes whiter*. In other words the subject of *wash* can be not only the 'actor' (*She*) or the 'goal' (*the fabric*), but also the 'instrument' (*Brand X*). It has been suggested that we might look at these features in terms of 'case'. The point of this suggestion is that it takes account of the fact that such 'cases' are not formally marked in any uniform way and that we can (and should) look at the ways in which they are handled in English and other languages. This is an interesting piece of speculation, but it has nothing to do with grammatical case in our sense, beyond the fact that some of the distinctions we might need ('agent', 'object', 'instrument') are marked formally in some languages by case endings. But there will be more on this in 5.4.

2.6 Concord and government

In the first chapter we discussed the now traditional but rather unsatisfactory classification of languages into three types – inflected, agglutinative and isolating. The first two, inflected and agglutinative languages, share the characteristic that in both there are different forms of the same word (using 'word' in the sense we discussed on p. 49). It follows that in such languages there must often be choice between the forms of a word. Why do we have *likes* rather than *like* in English, *petite* rather than *petit* in French, *amamus* rather than *amatis* in Latin?

Sometimes the choice is free; for instance, we can choose between the present and the past tense forms of the verbs in the sentences:

> *The boy likes ice-cream,*
> *The boy liked ice-cream.*

These are of course different in meaning but the choice of *likes* and *liked* is not determined by anything in the sentence.

By contrast with the sentences above there is no freedom of choice between the forms of the verb in:

>*The boy likes ice-cream,*
>*The boys like ice-cream.*

Although we have again two forms of the verb LIKE, the choice is determined by the occurrence of *boy* and *boys*. What is important is that *boy* and *likes* occur together as do *boys* and *like*, and that if we pair them wrongly we shall produce a sentence that will be immediately recognized as ungrammatical. There is clearly a grammatical restriction involving the morpho-syntactic category of number.

In the traditional grammars these restrictions are dealt with under two headings, concord (or agreement) and government. Both are very clearly exemplified in Latin; this is hardly surprising since their justification rests largely on the requirements of Latin grammar.

Let us first consider concord. In Latin a verb is said to agree with its subject (a noun or a pronoun) in person and number and an adjective is said to agree in number, gender and case with the noun it modifies. Agreement of the verb with its subject in number is shown by:

>*puer venit*   'the boy comes'
>*pueri veniunt* 'the boys come'

The singular noun form *puer* requires a singular verb form *venit*, while the plural *pueri* requires the plural *veniunt*, and the verb is said to agree in number, singular or plural, with the noun. Similarly, we may compare the second example above with:

>*nos venimus* 'we come'
>*vos venitis*   'you (plural) come'

The difference now is one of person – first person, second person or third person – and again the choice of the verb form depends on the subject (which in these two examples is a pronoun). The verb is said, then, to agree with the pronoun in person (as well as in number). There are similar examples in French, German, Italian, Spanish and other languages. In French, for example, we have:

>*le garçon vient* 'the boy comes'
>*les garçons viennent* 'the boys come'

In French, incidentally, though there are often five different forms for any one tense of the written language, there are frequently only three different forms in the spoken language, e.g.:

(*je*) *chante*	ʃãt	'I sing'
(*tu*) *chantes*	ʃãt	'you sing'
(*il*) *chante*	ʃãt	'he sings'
(*nous*) *chantons*	ʃãtɔ	'we sing'
(*vous*) *chantez*	ʃãte	'you sing'
(*ils*) *chantent*	ʃãt	'they sing'

Only the 'we' and 'you' forms differ from the rest.

In English there are two forms only: *comes* which occurs with *he*, *she*, *it* and all singular nouns, and *come* which occurs with all the other pronouns. Clearly there is still concord, but we surely do not need to talk about concord in terms of person as well as number. We do not, that is to say, want to make all the distinctions of first, second and third person as well as singular and plural, when there are only two possible forms of the verb. The fact is simply that there is one form for the third person singular and another for the rest. We should be wise to hesitate before setting up such a complex system to deal with just two forms.

To illustrate in full the agreement of adjectives with nouns in Latin we should need to write out the whole number, gender and case paradigm to produce thirty-six ($2 \times 3 \times 6$) forms in all. But a brief illustration can be provided by taking one adjective-noun sequence and contrasting it with three other such sequences differing each in number, gender and case respectively:

vir bonus	'the good man'
viri boni	'the good men' (number: plural)
mulier bona	'a good woman' (gender: feminine)
viro bono	'to a good man' (case: dative)

The situation in German and Russian is similar to that in Latin, though there are fewer cases in German. In the Romance languages there are no cases, but there is agreement in number and gender, as in Italian:

| *l'uomo buono* | 'the good man' |
| *gli uomini buoni* | 'the good men' |

| *la donna buona* | 'the good lady' |
| *le donne buone* | 'the good ladies' |

In French the pattern is clear only in the written language, for in the spoken language many of the contrasts are lost (see p. 33). It should be noted too that in the Italian examples the articles are also involved in the agreement. This is also true of French, Spanish and German, and in German it is a matter of case as well as number and gender:

| *der gute Mann* | 'the good man' |
| *des guten Mannes* | 'of the good man' (genitive) |

Nothing similar exists in English.

Let us now turn to government. In Latin, prepositions and verbs are said to govern nouns in a certain case. Thus *a* ('from') governs nouns in the ablative while *ad* ('to') governs nouns in the accusative:

| *a monte* | 'from the mountain' |
| *ad montem* | 'to the mountain' |

Similarly, some verbs govern the objects in the accusative, others in the genitive, others in the dative and still others in the ablative:

hominem videre	'to see a man' (accusative)
hominis meminisse	'to remember a man' (genitive)
homini parere	'to obey a man' (dative)
gladio uti	'to use a sword' (ablative)

In languages such as English and French it is doubtful whether this concept of government can be usefully applied. Case can be established only for the pronouns and then only a system of two cases, nominative and accusative – *I/me, he/him, we/us, je/me, il/le*, etc. But the distinction does not depend on the verb, since there is no variation with different verbs, but only on the grammatical function of subject and object. The point is quite simply that with pronouns there is one form for the subject and another for the object. There is little value in talking about verbs governing their objects in the accusative if this is the only case in which they govern nouns. There is, indeed, no more reason for talking about verbs governing their objects in the accusative than of verbs governing their subjects in the nominative (and this has been suggested), since the choice of case does not depend on the verb, but the function of the pronoun in the sentence. In French the position is slightly more complicated as there are three pronoun forms for some pronouns, e.g. *il/le/lui*, but again the choice does not depend on the verb but on the function of the pronoun.

As was suggested earlier, this whole dichotomy of agreement and government is a product of Latin grammar. Verbs and adjectives are said to agree with nouns, but nouns are said to be governed by prepositions and verbs. Why this distinction? Is it that where the noun is the determining factor we speak of agreement, where its form is determined we speak of government? This is not quite the answer. In the examples of government it is clear that we have the form of a noun determined by a particular verb or class of verb (not a form of a verb). Thus the verb PAREO 'obey' (in all its forms) takes the dative, i.e. requires a dative form of a noun. On the other hand, where there is agreement in number and case between adjective and noun we find that one form of a noun requires the corresponding form (i.e. with the same number and case) of an adjective:

vir bonus	'a good man' (both nominative singular)
viros bonos	'good men' (both accusative plural)

We have a clear distinction, then, between two kinds of linkage: (1) of a word or class of word requiring a particular form of another word and (2) a form of one word requiring a corresponding form of another. The labels 'government' and 'agreement' would seem to be applicable to these two situations respectively, but this will involve some modification of traditional practice. For instance, it is usually said that French adjectives agree with nouns in number and gender as in:

le bon garçon	'the good boy'
les bons garçons	'the good boys'
la bonne fille	'the good girl'
les bonnes filles	'the good girls'

There is clearly agreement in number in our sense; a particular form of the noun requires a particular form of the adjective – both forms must be either singular or plural. But with gender this is not so. It is a word, the lexical item for 'boy' or for 'girl', and not any particular form of the word, that requires a particular form of the adjective, either masculine or feminine. But this is not agreement on our definition, but government. We ought to say, then, that in French nouns govern the adjectives for gender.

Often government and agreement (in our precise sense) are involved in the linkage of identical items. An example would be the Latin:

viro bono paruit.   'He obeyed the good man.'

Here we must say that:

(1) the verb (*paruit*) governs the noun (*viro*) in case (dative).

(2) the adjective (*bono*) agrees with the noun in case.

(3) the adjective also agrees with the noun in number (singular).

(4) the noun governs the adjective in gender (masculine).

This may seem complicated because to account for the number and case of *bono* we have to talk about agreement with the noun (whose case is determined by government by the verb), while the gender of the adjective is determined by government by the noun. No wonder, one may think, traditional grammar did not use the terms 'government' and 'agreement' in this way. But the distinction is important because government in our sense involves the lexicon while agreement does not: if a particular verb requires a particular case, or a particular noun requires a certain gender form of the adjective, this has to be indicated in the dictionary. We have to show that Latin PAREO takes the dative or that French TABLE requires *la* and not *le*, or *petite* and not *petit*. Inconsistently, the dictionaries talk about TABLE being feminine but do not talk about PAREO being dative, though the position is exactly the same; in both instances the characterization of the class of noun or verb to which they belong is that they require a particular form of another word somewhere in the sentence.

What happens in Latin is not, of course, typical of all other languages. We find different grammatical categories involved in what seem to be conditions similar to those of Latin or the European languages. For instance, we have noted that the verb agrees with the noun-subject in number, with further (and more complex) relations with pronouns in terms of person. In many languages, however, gender as well as number and person is involved in the relations between the noun and the verb. This is particularly true of the Semitic and Cushitic languages (see pp. 79–80). A feminine noun will be accompanied by a feminine form of the verb. Moreover, the second and third person pronouns are distinguished for gender and also require appropriate forms of the verb. Oddly enough, the first person pronouns are not so distinguished; apparently there is less need to indicate gender when referring to oneself. It has been suggested that gender is a concord feature even in French, in its spoken form at least, as in:

> *le garçon travaille-t-il?*
> *la jeune fille travaille-t-elle?*

For we could quite reasonably regard the pronoun here as part of the verb (or its suffix). On that interpretation we have here an example of the noun governing the verb in gender.

In the Semitic languages the verbs often have two kinds of endings, one relating to the subject, the other to the object, so that they can be simultaneously governed by or agree with two different nouns, the subject and the object. In the examples below we illustrate government in gender by both subject and object in Tigrinya:

Subject	Object	Verb	
säb'äy	*nəsäb'äy*	*qätiluwo*	'The man killed the man'
säb'äy	*nəsäbäyti*	*qätiluwa*	'The man killed the woman'
säbäyti	*nəsäb'äy*	*qätilätto*	'The woman killed the man'
säbäyti	*nəsäbäyti*	*qätilätta*	'The woman killed the woman'

Further examples would show agreement of the verb with both subject and object in number. The forms of the verb with plural subjects and objects would be *qätilomwom, qätilomwän, qatilänom, qatilän'än.*

Sometimes it is not the category involved that is strange by European standards, but the grammatical construction. In some languages, for instance, there is government in the possessor/possessed (genitive) construction of the kind exemplified by *the boy's book.* We have already seen what happens in Bilin (see p. 65). In effect, a genitive form in Bilin is treated exactly as though it were an adjective, and is declined like one. It is, therefore, governed by the noun in gender and agrees with it in case and number. It is worth noting perhaps that some traditional grammars of Latin suggested that the genitive was par excellence the adjectival case.

The Bilin example follows the European pattern, although it involves a new kind of government and concord, in that it is the possessor which is marked: the word for 'man's' is the form in the 'genitive', as it would seem to be in English and as it certainly is in Latin. In some languages, however, it is the possessed noun that carries the mark to indicate the construction. It is as if in English we said *The boy book-his*. If this were, in fact, the English form, *his* would exhibit government in gender and agreement in number with the noun *boy*. A real example is to be found in Menomini, an Amerindian language, where 'that man's dog' is represented by *enoh enε·wih oti·hsεhsan* but 'those men's dogs' is *akohenε·niwak oti·hsehsowa·wan*. The last words are the words for 'dog' or rather for 'dog-his' and 'dog-their'. The form of these depends on the number of the preceding noun, the possessor, for the possessor noun governs the possessed noun in number.

It is clear from previous chapters that the grammatical categories that are involved in government and agreement have very little exact meaning. What, then, is the function of government and agreement? What information do they provide? One answer is that they often provide little or no information and are almost completely redundant. French would be no less intelligible, and would certainly be easier to learn, if we did not have to bother with the gender and the number of adjectives, if in fact its adjectives followed the same pattern as those of English. For although the gender and number of an adjective is an indication of the structure to which it belongs (an adjective is thus identified as modifying a certain noun), this relationship is already indicated by the position of the adjective – i.e. before or after the noun. We do not therefore need its gender and number to establish that relationship. Thus, in languages where there is a fairly fixed order of words, and where that order indicates the grammatical relations between the words, concord and government would appear to be unnecessary luxuries (or difficulties). By contrast, in Latin, and especially Latin verse, the order of the words is not fixed and the concord-government patterns are all important in establishing the grammatical structure. In Virgil for instance we find (the opening words of the *Eclogues*):

> *Tityre tu patulae recubans sub tegmine fagi*
> *silvestrem tenui musam meditaris avena.*

But this cannot be understood unless we note that *patulae* goes with *fagi*, *silvestrem* with *musam* and *tenui* with *avena*. That they do is clear from their number, gender and case.

This of course explains why number is not directly associated with counting or gender with sex. Part of the function of these categories (sometimes the major part of their function) is to indicate syntactic relations – that an adjective and a noun together form a single phrase or that a noun is the subject or object of a verb. Where such functions are clearly marked in other ways these categories become redundant and are often lost, as gender has been lost in English.

3 Morphology

Grammar is traditionally divided into morphology and syntax. Morphology is essentially the grammar of words and deals with the forms of words, the relation between *take* and *took*, *dog* and *dogs*. Syntax is the grammar of sentences and is concerned with the way that sentences are formed (often largely in terms of words).

Until the last few decades morphology had attracted the greater interest, especially among structuralists (see 3.1 and 4.1); it is even assumed sometimes, in popular thought, that grammar is morphology (p. 13). In recent years, however, attention has turned to syntax while morphology has been rather neglected; this is reflected in the comparison of the length of this chapter with the combined length of the next two.

3.1 Morphemes

For reasons that we discussed in the previous chapter, many linguists, particularly in America, came to the conclusion that the word was not, or at least not necessarily, the basic unit of grammar, but that often we have to look to something smaller than the word. This idea is clearly stated by Bloomfield. He pointed out that there are linguistic forms which are never heard in isolation (and so are not words by his definition); these he called *bound* forms. His examples were the -*y* (/i/) of Johnny and Billy and the -*ing* (/iŋ/) of *singing* and *dancing*. These are clearly linguistic forms since they 'are phonetic forms . . . with constant meaning'. These forms he called MORPHEMES. His precise definition of a morpheme is 'a linguistic form that bears no partial phonetic-semantic resemblance to any other form'. This rather forbidding negative definition is in reality quite simple. By 'bears no partial . . . resemblance' he meant that no part of it had any resemblance. To obtain the morphemes, then, we must divide up our linguistic forms until no part of any one is similar to any other in both its phonetic and its semantic characteristics. Thus *dancing* cannot be a morpheme because part of it resembles the first part of *dances* and part of it resembles the second part of *singing*. But if we divide *dancing* into two – *danc-* (/dæns/) and *ing* (/iŋ/) – these forms have no partial resemblance to any other forms and, therefore, are morphemes.

At first sight the usefulness of the concept of the morpheme is obvious. We can treat *singing* and *dancing* each as two morphemes but with an identical second morpheme *-ing*, and we can similarly analyse *danced* and *loved* or *cats* and *bricks*. We must simply divide up the 'complex' forms of language until we arrive at these 'simple' forms (and Bloomfield used the term 'simple' for morphemes). The remaining task of the grammarian is simply to state all the possible combinations of these simple forms.

It is obvious that this kind of analysis works admirably for the agglutinative languages (see p. 52) and that any reasonable grammars of such languages should be along these lines. Our Swahili example *alikuona* (p. 51) consists of the elements (i.e. morphemes) *a*, *li*, *ku* and *ona*. We may well ask, however, whether such an approach is suitable for the inflectional languages. Is it not precisely because they do not lend themselves to this type of analysis that they differ from the agglutinative ones? In the Greek example we considered (see p. 52) *lusontai* can be divided into six morphemes but can *luo:*?

The morpheme was not, however, for Bloomfield, the smallest element of language. For morphemes consist of PHONEMES; the morpheme *-ing*, for instance, consists of the phonemes /i/ and /ŋ/. To understand this, we must look briefly at the theoretical basis of Bloomfield's views. These views, and more particularly those of his successors, the 'post-Bloomfieldians', are usually described as 'structuralism', or, strictly, as 'American structuralism'. As the name suggests, the main thesis is that language has a structure. In a general sense, of course, all linguists are structuralists in that they look for regularities, patterns or rules in language. But for this school of linguistics, language structure was of a very specific kind. In particular, it was made up of morphemes and of phonemes. Phonemes are the sounds or strictly the distinctive sounds of language – *cat* consists of the phonemes /k/, /æ/ and /t/, *tough* of the phonemes /t/, /ʌ/ and /f/[1]; an explanation of the morpheme is to come. These are both units of form, not of meaning, though there was considerable

1. It is a convention to use slant lines to indicate phonemes, italics being used for a script that is either an orthography (e.g. Swahili) or a transliteration (e.g. Greek). For many languages the script is sufficiently phonemic to be used as a basis for morphological analysis without a phonemic transcription.

controversy among linguists about the question as to whether morphemes should or should not be considered as having meaning. The essential sense, however, in which the approach is structural is that the language is supposed to be actually composed of morphemes in sequence, i.e. of 'strings' of morphemes and similarly, though at a different level, of strings of phonemes. Morphemes in general are larger than phonemes; in fact they are composed of phonemes, it being a requirement that a morpheme must consist of one or more phonemes. Thus *singing* would be said to be made up of the phonemes /s/, /i/, /ŋ/, /i/ and /ŋ/ and of the morphemes *sing-* (or /siŋ/) and *-ing* (or /iŋ/). To establish this morphemic and phonemic structure the linguist must establish first of all what the morphemes and phonemes of the language are by segmenting and classifying actual language material, and then must see clearly what combination of units of the same kind may occur (this is known as 'tactics') and how the morphemes are made up of phonemes. It was recognized that there must be units larger than the morpheme, though these were never very clearly defined (see p. 12). But here again the same principles would apply; language would actually consist of such units and it was the task of the linguist to establish what they were and how they related to one another and to the other (smaller) units of the language.

An attempt, however, to deal with morphology in these terms runs into difficulties. There are many problems that any student of morphology must face, and some of these can best be illustrated by looking, in some detail, at the various modifications that had to be made to Bloomfield's original morpheme. Many of them Bloomfield had to make himself – even in *Language* it is not held to be strictly true that 'morphemes consist of phonemes':

(1) Bloomfield found it necessary to talk of 'alternants'. His example was that of the plural form in English which even when written with an *-s* nevertheless has three phonological shapes:

/iz/	in	*horses*
/z/	in	*dogs*
/s/	in	*cats*

Other examples show that /iz/ appears after sibilants and palato-alveolar consonants (*glasses*, *roses*, *dishes*, *garages*, *churches*, *bridges*); /z/ appears after all other voiced phonemes (*saws*, *boys*, *ribs*, *sleeves*, *pens*, *hills*, *cars*), and /s/ after all other voiceless phonemes (*books*, *cliffs*). There is a very similar situation with the past tense morpheme which has three phonological shapes /t/, /d/ and /id/ as in *liked*, *loved* and *hated* respectively (/id/ occurring only after /t/ and /d/). Alternants of this kind Bloomfield called 'phonetic alternants' because they 'can be described in terms of phonetic modification'. Later linguists used the term 'allomorph' (or simply 'morph') to designate the alternants, reserving the term morpheme for the whole class of alternants. Thus the plural morpheme {s} (with braces to show that it is a morpheme) would be said to have the allomorphs /iz/, /z/ and /s/ (with slant lines to show that these allomorphs consist of phonemes). This particular kind of alternation, moreover, was described by them as 'phonologically determined alternation' since it is determined by the phonological characteristics of the environment. We should perhaps not be surprised that morphemes should undergo 'phonetic modification' as Bloomfield called it. It is a very common characteristic of language that one sound seems to determine the nature of another adjacent sound. This happens even in agglutinative languages. In Swahili, for instance, *m* 'him' is replaced by *mw* before vowels:

a – li – m – penda	'he loved him'
a – li – mw – ona	'he saw him'

The introduction of the notion of alternants or allomorphs may seem, then, to be justified, but it carries one important consequence. We can no longer say that morphemes consist of phonemes, but rather that the allomorphs or alternants consist of phonemes. However plausible this modification may be it radically changes the model. (In 3.2 we shall consider a different model, that deals with this problem in a more satisfying way.)

(2) Bloomfield also noted that there are irregular alternants. His examples were the first part of:

knife	/naif/	*knives*	/naiv-z/
mouth	/mauθ/	*mouths*	/mauð-z/
house	/haus/	*houses*	/hauz-iz/

These are irregular because the final consonant is voiceless in the singular form and voiced in the plural – /f/ changes to /v/, /θ/ to /ð/, and /s/ to /z/. This does not occur with most of the other words that end in the same consonants; we must contrast *cliffs*, *myths* and *creases*. There are other words with plurals similar to *knives* and *mouths* (e.g. *wives*, *wreaths*), but *houses* is in this respect quite idiosyncratic: there is no other plural form in the English language which involves an /s/ – /z/ alternation with an /iz/ ending.

More striking is the plural form of *ox* – *oxen*. Bloomfield described the ending (/ən/) as 'suppletive', and it is clear that on his definition this must be a different morpheme from that represented by /s/, /z/ and /iz/. Most later linguists concluded that it was an allomorph of the same morpheme, and referred to this kind of alternation as 'morphologically conditioned alternation' because it was conditioned by the occurrence of a particular preceding (or, where appropriate, following) morpheme, and not by any phonological feature. However, with morphologically conditioned allomorphs, not only is a morpheme not composed of phonemes (though its alternants may be), but also there is no simple explanation of the alternation as there is for the phonologically conditioned allomorphs. It should be noted, too, that phonological and morphological conditioning are not alternatives. Many morphemes are both morphologically and phonologically conditioned. Thus the occurrence of /iz/ is morphologically conditioned in that it occurs with *glass*, *horse*, *crease*, etc., but not with *ox*, and phonologically conditioned in terms of the preceding sibilant or affricate.

(3) In view of the fact that the plural of *sheep* is identical with that of the singular form, and that the same is true for the spoken form of *postman* (/pousmən/, see p. 31), Bloomfield also talked about 'zero' alternants and later scholars of 'zero' allomorphs. It was thought that morphemes have zero allomorphs, though with the condition that zero cannot be the only allomorph of a morpheme. This prevents the establishment of, for instance, a morpheme {singular} in English, since that would have zero as its only allomorph. This is reasonable if morphemes are linguistic forms. Yet the notion of a zero allomorph in *sheep* (plural) and *hit* (past tense), although obviously very useful, still does not wholly fit Bloomfield's definition. A zero element cannot really be said to have 'no partial phonetic-semantic resemblance to any other form'.

(4) The converse of the zero allomorph or morph is what Hockett called the 'empty morph'. Sometimes in a language we find some phonological material that seems to belong to no morpheme at all. Hockett's examples were taken from an American Indian language, but there is one possible example in

English. The plural form of *child* is *children* – phonemically /tʃildrən/. It is reasonable to regard /tʃaild/ in the singular and /tʃild/ in the plural as allomorphs of the same morpheme, and it is equally reasonable to identify the /ən/ with the /ən/ of *oxen*. What then can we say of the /r/? It is an 'empty' morph, since it belongs to no morpheme at all. However useful, the empty morph again cannot easily be related to Bloomfield's morpheme.

(5) Bloomfield also had to consider the analysis of such forms as *geese*, *men*, *took*, *knew*, as compared with *goose*, *man*, *take* and *know*. These he treated in terms of 'substitution alternants'. The substitution of /iː/ in *geese* or of /e/ in *men* for /uː/ and /æ/ respectively is, he said, an alternant of the normal singular suffix. A similar suggestion appears in later works where to account for *took* (/tuk/) as compared with *take* (/teik/), we have the replacive allomorph /u←ei/ or /ei~ u/ – i.e. '/u/ replaces /ei/' or 'change /ei/ to /u/'. But it is immediately obvious that this is a very strange allomorph; an instruction to replace one item by another can hardly be regarded as in any sense consisting of phonemes.

(6) Hockett had a different solution for the same problem – /tuk/ is a 'portmanteau' morph, one that belongs simultaneously to two morphemes – *take* and *ed*. This, of course, preserves the notion that morphemes consist of phonemes, but with the reservation that individual morphemes do not always consist of phonemes, but that two or more morphemes jointly may be said to consist of phonemes. This solution is more plausible in those cases where the morphemes also have other allomorphs that are not portmanteaux. We may compare /tuk/ with /lʌvd/ (*loved*) which is clearly divisible into /lʌv/ and /d/, and since /lʌvd/ is two morphemes, it can be argued that /tuk/ is too. It is much less plausible to apply a similar analysis to the endings of the Latin verb such as the *o* of *amo*; such a portmanteau would have to belong to five different morphemes, those of first person, singular, present, indicative and active. These morphemes never seem to have their own separate allomorphs, but are always 'fused'. But the notion of the morpheme as a recognizable unit with a phonetic and semantic 'shape' can hardly be maintained, if all the forms are portmanteaux.

(7) Bloomfield also suggested that we might have 'minus' features. The best known example is in the French adjective. For many words the difference between the masculine and the

feminine form is that the feminine has an extra consonant or
consonants (see pp. 32–3). Some of Bloomfield's examples are:

plat	/pla/	*platte*	/plat/	'flat'
laid	/lɛ/	*laide*	/lɛd/	'ugly'
distinct	/distɛ̃/	*distincte*	/distɛ̃kt/	'distinct'

We should wish to say that the final /t/ of /plat/ is dropped or
deleted in the masculine rather than say that /t/ is added to
/pla/ to form the feminine, for the latter solution would involve
us in setting up a motley collection of consonants to be added as
allomorphs of the morpheme {feminine}. Since the consonant
varies from word to word it is far easier to suppose that the
feminine form is the basic form and that the masculine form
loses its final consonant or consonants, than to treat the many
different final consonants as marks of the feminine. A little
reflection will show that this is a very strange concept indeed if
we are thinking in Bloomfield's terms. How can a minus feature
be composed of phonemes?

Within the various viewpoints we have been considering, a
number of solutions are possible for the same linguistic form.
For instance, at least six interpretations of the relation of *take*
and *took* can be given:

(a) *Take* and *took* are different (single) morphemes. This is
perhaps the only real solution as a strict interpretation of
Bloomfield's original concept, but it loses the important gener-
alization that these words are comparable to *bake* and *baked*;
the latter must surely consist of *bake-* /beik/ and *-d* /t/.
Moreover, is it true that *take* and *took* have 'no partial phonetic–semantic resemblance'? Their initial and final consonants
are the same.

(b) *Take* and *took* are each two morphemes, with the shared
allomorph /t . . k/ and further allomorphs /ei/ and /u/. This has
the great advantage of identifying the shared part of the two
forms, the /t/ and /k/ within one morpheme, and so preserving
Bloomfield's notion of 'phonetic forms'. It is attractive, moreover, because a similar analysis seems essential in some languages, e.g. Arabic where the consonants form the 'roots' and
the vowels are part of the purely grammatical elements. Thus in
kataba 'he wrote', *kutiba* 'it was written', it would seem that
{k . . t . . b} is the morpheme 'write'. But this solution again
destroys the parallelism with *bake* and *baked* for the former is

usually to be regarded as one morpheme and the latter as two, the first morpheme plus *d*.

(c) *Take* is one morpheme, *took* two; /tuk/ is a portmanteau morph.

(d) *Take* is one morpheme, *took* two; *took* consists of the morphs /teik/ and /u←ei/.

(e) *Take* is one morpheme, *took* two; *took* consists of two morphs, /tuk/ which is an allomorph of (take) and zero (/ø/) which is an allomorph of·{d}. This is perhaps the best solution within the theory since it retains the pattern of *bake/baked*: *baked* consists of two morphemes in sequence – first the morpheme {bake} and then the morpheme {d}. *Took* similarly on this analysis consists of two morphemes – {take} and {d}, but with allomorphs /tuk/ and /ø/. There is one curious point, however; /tuk/ is a morphologically conditioned allomorph occurring in the immediate environment of {d} which is here /ø/, /teik/ occurs where there is no following {d}. If we think how we can recognize the morphs, we appear to be saying that /tuk/ occurs before zero, and /teik/ before nothing!

(f) *Take* is one morpheme and *took* two; *took* consists of /t . . k/ which is an allomorph of *take* and /u/ which is an allomorph of /d/ (the other allomorph of *take* being, in the present form, /teik/). This seems one of the least plausible of all the solutions because it treats the vowels of the two forms in totally different ways.

3.2 Morphological processes

The problems that were discussed in the last section involve the complex relations between the morphemic and the phonemic patterns of a language, and are, therefore, matters of MORPHO-PHONEMICS. There are, however, some curious inconsistencies in the proposals made there. The notions of alternants and of phonetic modification are not entirely compatible, while there is even greater inconsistency in both treating morphemes and morphs or allomorphs as composed of phonemes and talking about change, substitution and subtraction. Morphology should either be a matter of alternate forms, e.g. *knife* and *knive-*, or concerned with the ways that one form may be changed into another, e.g. of changing the voiceless /f/ of *knife* into the voiced /v/ of *knives*. In a well-known article, 'Two models of grammatical description', Hockett suggested that there are two essentially different approaches to morphology, IA ('Item and Arrangement') and IP ('Item and Process'). The first was adopted, in theory at least, by the structuralists, as we have already seen; the second is an older, more traditional model, and although this is not always acknowledged, it is the model now used in 'generative phonology', the phonological– morphological approach adopted in transformational generative grammar (see p. 156). Hockett pointed out that many of the devices suggested by the structuralists were not strictly permissible in an IA model. /ei→u/ is not a morph at all, for it is not composed of phonemes; it is an instruction to make a change. The same is true of subtractive (minus) features. There would be no problem about either of these in an IP model; they are simply some of the processes or changes that the model uses. Thus we can say that the past tense of *take* is formed by changing the vowel /ei/ of the present to /u/, and that French masculine adjectives are formed by deleting the final consonant of the feminine forms. Of course, both alternation and process can be used in a single model. IP need not rule out alternation as one type of process, but IA, on the other hand, rules out process by definition.

It may seem strange that anyone should object to such a simple and traditional idea as 'change', but the structuralists certainly did object. Hockett himself was worried by the notion, and felt that it might imply that the change took place in time. For linguists have for a long time distinguished between synchronic and diachronic descriptions, the former dealing with a language as it is at any particular time, the latter with the history of the language, and they have been critical of scholars who confuse the two. But this is not a serious point. We can talk metaphorically of synchronic change, change that describes a language, without implying that this change takes place or took place in time either in the history of the language or even in the brains of the speakers; it is merely a descriptive device to say that *took* 'changes' into *take*, just like saying that two and two 'make' four. Indeed we can write morphophonemic rules such as /ei→u/ to account for *take* and *took*, or C→ø ('a consonant becomes zero') to show that the final consonant of the feminine form of an adjective in French may be deleted to produce the masculine. (On the status of such rules see p. 129.)

In a sense, IA allows one type of process, that of addition. We may add -s to *cat*. But we may not 'change' this -s (/s/) to produce the -s (/z/) of *dogs*; we merely note that there are alternative forms. This model ideally fits agglutinative languages; indeed it seems almost to suggest that agglutination is the only proper kind of morphological formation. By contrast inflectional languages are more simply dealt with in IP. A process approach allows much greater freedom of description because all kinds of process are permissible. It also allows us to deal much more plausibly with Bloomfield's 'phonetic modification'. For such modification can best be seen as a change; moreover, the implication is that the change is in some way motivated, that it comes about because of the phonetic environment (see p. 102). A fairly simple example is found in Classical Greek. There are nominative and genitive forms of nouns such as the following:

gú:ps	gu:pós	'vulture'
pʰléps	pʰlebós	'vein'
pʰúlaks	pʰúlakos	'sentry'
aíks	aigós	'goat'

Clearly the ending for the nominative is -s and for the genitive -os, and the stems of the words for 'vulture' and 'sentry' are gu:p- and pʰulak-. But for the other words there is a choice between pʰlep- and pʰleb-, and between aik- and aig-. The simplest explanation of these is that the stem is pʰleb- and aig-, and that the voiced consonants b and g become voiceless p and k before the voiceless s of the nominative. Changes such as this are known as SANDHI (a word taken from the Indian grammarians). Moreover, the modification that is involved here is one of ASSIMILATION – the voiced consonants are assimilated in terms of their voicing with the voiceless -s.

There is another important point. If the assimilation had not taken place, the resultant form would have been phonologically impossible in Classical Greek. For that language does not permit voiced plosives such as b and g to occur before s. The variation is, then, in a sense, forced by the phonology of the language. Such variations are known as AUTOMATIC. There is a possible alternative solution that sees the change as going in the opposite direction – from voiceless consonants to voiced ones rather than from voiced to voiceless. This would say that the voiceless p and k before s become voiced b and g when inter-vocalic (between two vowels). But in that solution, the variation is not automatic, because voiceless plosives are permitted between vowels in Greek; moreover, it would wrongly predict that the genitive forms of the other two words should be *pʰúlagos and *gu:bós.

The direction of the change is obvious enough in the Greek examples. It is less obvious with the *-s* plural endings of English. Here we have /-s/ (*cats*), /-z/ (*dogs*) and /-iz/ (*horses*). Once again we have assimilation (with the first two alternants), since /-s/ occurs in the environment of voiceless sounds and /-z/ in the environment of voiced ones. But, whereas in Greek the consonant assimilates in terms of voicing with a following sound, (REGRESSIVE assimilation), in the English examples it assimilates with the previous sound (PROGRESSIVE assimilation). With /-iz/ we have a rather different phenomenon, but nevertheless one that can be explained in phonetic and phonological terms. The presence of /i/ ensures that the /s/ or /z/ is kept apart from similar sounds – /s/, /z/, /ʃ/, /ʒ/, /tʃ/ and /dʒ/. (Only the *-s* of plural forms will be discussed here, but exactly the same remarks may be made of possessive forms (*cat's*, *dog's*, *horse's*) and of the *-s* forms of verbs (*hits*, *digs*, *suffices*) and even of the reduced forms of *is* – see below.

Which of these three alternants is to be taken as the basic one, the one that changes into the others? The spelling would suggest /s/, but spelling is not a good guide, and, inconsistently, the spelling has *-ed* for the past tense where very similar processes are at work (see p. 110). If we take /s/ as basic the changes will not be automatic, for /s/ does not have to change into /z/ after voiced consonants to preserve the phonological pattern: for English as the words *fence* (/fens/), *hence* (/hens/) and *else* (/els/) where a voiceless /s/ follows a voiced /n/ or /l/. We may contrast *fence* (/fens/) with *fens* (/fenz/), and similarly *hence* with *hens*, *else* with *els*. If there is a restriction on the occurrence of /s/ with voiced consonants, it applies only to the grammatical endings and not generally in the language. We could, of course, simply say that the change is not automatic – that it applies only to *-s* endings, but is not determined wholly by the phonology. However, if we take /z/ as basic the change becomes automatic, because /z/ never occurs after a voiceless consonant in English. We need a further automatic change – that of inserting /i/ after /s/, /z/, etc. for words like *horses*, *churches*, *judges*. Alternatively, we could argue that /iz/ is basic, as Bloomfield does, and that the /i/ is deleted when the ending does not follow one of these consonants. That would allow us to deal in the same way with the reduced forms of the verb *is*. This is clearly /iz/ in its full form, but becomes /s/ or /z/ in exactly the same way as the plural *-s*, as in:

The cat's (/kæts/) *in the basket.*
The dog's (dɔgz/) *in the kennel.*
The horse is (/hɔːsiz/) *in the stable.*

If the rules are stated fairly generally they apply also to the past tense form *ed*:

liked	/laikt/
loved	/lʌvd/
batted	/bætid/

The /i/ is inserted (or deleted) where the consonants are similar; otherwise there is assimilation in terms of voicing. Yet English writes *-ed*, not *-t* (analogously, why not write *-ez* instead of *-s*?). There is something inconsistent about writing *licks* with *-s* and *licked* with *-ed* when the phenomena are virtually the same. The reason English is so inconsistent lies in the complexities of the spelling, which are fairly consistent in their own internal conventions, but not directly based on pronunciation.

Not all variation is automatic. In English the past tense forms of *burn* and *learn* are /bəːnt/ and /ləːnt/ with a final voiceless consonant (though the spelling allows both *learnt* and *learned*, *burnt* and *burned*). But there is no general phonetic reason; one would, rather, expect a voiced consonant to follow the voiced nasal /n/. Nor is there any reason in the phonology of English, since English permits /d/ after /n/ as in *find* or *sound*; the change is not, therefore, automatic. (By contrast the *-s* forms of these verbs conforms with the automatic pattern – /bəːnz/, /ləːnz/.)

'Automatic' must not be confused with 'regular'. A change or variation is said to be regular if it applies to most forms of the language, and, in particular, if it applies to new or invented forms. Examples of invented forms are *pibs*, *ropped* and *lishes* in the sentence on p. 12. Thus, the plural *-s* form is regular, whereas the *-en* in *oxen* is not. The variation between /s/, /z/ and /iz/ is regular too, and with no exceptions. The variation in the past tense between /t/, /d/ and /id/ is also regular, but not one hundred per cent, because of /bəːnt/, /ləːnt/, etc. Regularity is a matter of degree; there is a partial regularity in these forms of *burn* and *learn*, in that the /t/ variation is restricted to verbs ending in /n/ or /l/.

A regular change need not, then, be automatic. In Italian, for example, it is usually the case that a velar consonant will change to a palatal before a front vowel. Because this is regular it is not shown in the spelling as the following singular and plural forms illustrate:

amico (/amiːko/)   *amici* (/amiːtʃi/)   'friend'
astrologo (/astrologo/)   *astrologi* (/astrolodʒi/) 'astrologer'

But the variation is not automatic, for Italian allows front vowels after velars, even in plurals, where there is a change in the spelling with no direct phonetic significance:

fico (/fiːko/)   *fichi* (/fiːki/)   'fig'
luogo (/luogo/)   *luoghi* (/luogi/)   'place'

The linguist will, however, normally choose a solution, where possible, that treats a regular variation as automatic; that was precisely why we argued for /z/ rather than /s/ as the base form for English -*s*.

Conversely, automatic changes need not be regular. Let us reconsider *wife/wives* and *mouth* (/θ/) /*mouths* (/ð/), where the final consonant of the stem is voiced in the plural (p. 32). Now if the base form of -*s* is /z/, we can see that a change is required to conform with the phonological pattern, since /*waifz/ and /*mauθz/ would be impossible. The regular pattern of progressive assimilation would give /*waifs/ and /*mauθs/, with a change to /s/ (progressive assimilation). But regressive assimilation voices the final consonant of the stem to produce the forms that actually occur. Both types of assimilation 'solve' the phonological 'problem', and so are automatic, but only the first is regular. There is a curious variation in *house/houses* that is both irregular and non-automatic; the forms are /haus/ and /hauziz/, not /*hausiz/ as would be expected, and there is no explanation at all for the change of /s/ to /z/ in the stem (though the /iz/ ending is both automatic and regular).

A slightly more complex analysis is required for the past tense forms of English verbs such as *put*, *hit*, *set*. Since they are exactly the same as the present tense forms, the morphemic solution is to say that they have a zero (/ø/) allomorph of the past tense. But it is, perhaps, no coincidence that all of these verbs end in *t* or, less commonly, *d* (*bid*). It is possible, in fact, to treat this variation as automatic if we argue as follows. The usual ending /d/ would give /*putd/, and with the regular pattern an /i/ would be inserted to give /*putid/ (*putted* cf. *batted*). With this common set of verbs, however, the /i/ is not inserted. In that case the usual progressive assimilation would take place to give /*putt/. Then since English does not allow any geminates (double consonants), as many other languages do, one of the two /t/s is deleted to give the correct form /put/. This may seem a little involved, and may not even appear particularly plausible, but it does not invent any forms or any changes that cannot be regarded as motivated by the phonology. What is new is that we have two changes, or rules, one involving assimilation, one the deletion of a consonant. In generative phonology this idea of a sequence of rules is now a familiar one.

The fact that a change is forced by the phonology does not imply that we can always predict or infer what that change would be (though where a simple process such as assimilation takes place, it is, perhaps, reasonably inferrable). Indeed, the examples from the last two paragraphs show that there are two possible 'solutions' to problems created by the addition of the -s plural and -ed past tense affixes. In Italian a common ending for the past participle is -to as shown in the following infinitives and past participles:

morire	*morto*	'die'
spegnere	*spento*	'spend'
scegliere	*scelto*	'choose'
volgere	*volto*	'turn'

The first example raises no problems. In the next two we find that *gn* and *gl* (representing palatal nasals and laterals) change to *n* and *l*, their non-palatal counterparts. This change is automatic, since palatals do not occur before *t*. In the last example the change is certainly forced or motivated by the phonology, since *volgto* would be an impossible form. But there is no obvious way to predict that the form that the language 'chooses' is the one that simply omits the -*g*. There is a similar situation with forms that end in -*so* (another ending for the past participle):

apparire	*apparso*	'appear'
chiudere	*chiuso*	'close'
chiedere	*chiesto*	'call'
prendere	*preso*	'take'

The first involves no change. For the next two, change is forced because *chiudso* and *chiedso* would be impossible, but we cannot infer from the phonology that the forms would be as they are rather than, say, *chiusso* and *chiesso*. The change is motivated in the last example, too, since *prendso* would be impossible, but *prenso* with *d* omitted would conform to the pattern as well as the actual form *preso*.

In all the examples considered so far it has been possible to select one of a set of actually occurring forms as basic. But this is not always so if we wish to make a regular comprehensive analysis of a grammatical pattern. For instance, in Latin we have the nominative and genitive forms:

rex	*regis*	'king'
nox	*noctis*	'night'
nix	*nivis*	'snow'

The first is exactly like the Greek examples considered at the beginning of the section since *x* is phonologically /ks/ – the /g/ of the basic form is automatically devoiced by regressive assimilation. The second is only slightly more difficult: the stem /nokt/ would give a nominative /*nokts/, but the sequence of three consonants /kts/ is phonologically not permissible, and the middle /t/ is omitted. But the third example offers stems /nik/ and /niw/ (for *v* represents /w/), and there is no reason to suggest that /*niws/ would change to /niks/. Hockett suggests that the stem should be /*nigw-/, giving /*nigws/ and /*nigwis/. In the first the /w/ is omitted and the /g/ automatically devoiced to /k/; in the second the /g/ is omitted. In both cases the phonology would force the change, but what is changed is a non-occurring form. Hockett has a slightly more plausible example from the Amerindian language Potawatomi where the forms /pmos·e/ 'he's walking' and /npums·e/ 'I'm walking' occur; on the basis of comparison with other forms, we may say that the initial /n/ of the latter is first person ('I'), while the third person form ('he') has no prefix. But why the change from /pmos·e/ to /-pums·e/? Hockett suggests that the basic forms are /*nu-/ and /*pumos·e/, giving /*nupumos·e/ and /*pumos·e/. The syllabic structure of the language, however, requires a pattern of two consonants, then a vowel, then two consonants and so on. To conform, therefore, each alternate vowel, except the last, is deleted. On this analysis the change is automatic; it is in fact very plausible, because patterns of syllabic structure like this are found in other languages, e.g. colloquial

Arabic. But the basic forms do not exist independently; they are amalgams of actual forms.

Even within a small area of grammar in a single language the changes may involve all or most of the issues that have been raised. For instance, in one dialect of Oromo (Cushitic, Ethiopia) the present tense of the verb has such forms as:

bēka	'I know'
bēkta	'you (sing.) know'
bēkna	'we know'

Clearly the stem is *bēk-* and the endings -*a*, -*ta*, -*na*. But we also find:

qaba	'I take'
qabda	'you (sing.) take'
qabna	'we take'

Here -*ta* changes to -*da*; the change is automatic – *d* is assimilated (progressive assimilation) in terms of voicing to the preceding *b*. Then we have:

fida	'I carry'
fidda	'you (sing.) carry'
finna	'we carry'

Again -*ta* changes to -*da*, but the *d* of the stem changes to *n* before another *n*. The change is automatic, but the assimilation is now regressive, and in terms of nasality, not voice. Next consider:

gala	'I enter'	*fura*	'I redeem'
galta	'you (sing.) enter'	*furta*	'you (sing.) redeem'
galla	'we enter'	*furra*	'we redeem'

t does not now assimilate with the non-plosive but voiced consonants *l* and *r*, but *n* assimilates completely with *l* and *r*. All these changes are automatic, but not all are easily inferred.

Next, let us consider:

bu'a	'I climb'
būta	'you (sing.) climb'
būna	'we climb'

Here the glottal stop ' is dropped, but the vowel of the stem is lengthened before an ending beginning with a consonant. The facts are clear, the 'motivation' less so. This is also true of:

bāsa	'I extract'
bāfta	'you (sing.) extract'
bāfna	'we extract'

Why the change from *s* to *f*? Yet it appears to be completely regular (as does the alternation of ' and vowel length).

Finally, much less easy to explain is the pattern of:

gaa	'I arrive'
gēsa	'you (sing.) arrive'
gēña	'we arrive'

The simplest solution is to treat the stem as *gay-*. The *y* is deleted between two vowels to give *gaa*. Before a consonant, there are two changes. First, the following consonant is palatalized (*y* being palatal) – *s* being the palatal correlate of *t* and *ñ* of *n*. Secondly, *ay* becomes *ē* (this is quite a common change in other languages). The changes all appear to be motivated (but the analysis is complex), and depend on recognizing forms that do not occur. Finally, the reader may like to work out a solution for:

bēlaa	'I am famous'
bēlofta	'you (sing.) are famous'
bēlofna	'we are famous'

(Perhaps an underlying *-w-*?)

We must be careful about extending abstract analyses too far. It would be perfectly possible to invent a basic form for *take/took* – /*tʌik/. The present tense form /teik/ would be derived automatically because the sequence /ʌi/ does not occur, and the past tense form /tuk/ by changing /ʌ/ to /u/ and the deletion of /i/. But nothing at all is gained by such an artificial analysis. If we have abstract forms there must be some plausibility (or, as is sometimes said today, some 'naturalness'), both in the forms themselves and in the changes that take place. Yet, whenever there is a partial regularity, one is tempted to seek an explanation. For instance, in English we have a number of verbs of the pattern:

mean	(/miːn/)	*meant*	(/ment/)
lean	(/liːn/)	*leant*	(/lent/)
read	(/riːd/)	*read*	(/red/)
meet	(/miːt/)	*met*	(/met/)

In these there is a variation of the long vowel /iː/ and the short vowel /e/, and we find an exact parallel with the back vowels /uː/ and /ɔ/ in:

> *shoot*   (/ʃuːt/)   *shot*   (/ʃɔt/)

Now we could argue that, in general, the long vowels /iː/ and /uː/ do not occur before two consonants. (Exceptions are other grammatical forms that do not conform to this pattern such as *weaned*, -*s* forms in general, e.g. *leans*, *means*, *weans* and the word *fiend*; but the vowels never seem to occur before two consonants of which the second is /t/.) They are, therefore, replaced by the short vowels /e/ and /ɔ/, which are thus their morphophonemic counterparts, though not the phonetically most similar vowels, which are /i/ and /u/ as in *bit* and *put*. If so, the addition of the past tense ending /t/ would force the change with *mean* and *lean* (and it should be noted that it is /t/, as with *burn* and *learn*, not /d/). In the other cases we need several steps. First, the ending /d/ has to be added to give /*riːdd/, and with assimilation /*miːtt/ and /*ʃuːtt/. Then the vowels are shortened to give /*redd/, /*mett/ and /*ʃɔtt/, and finally the two consonants are reduced to one. This is only slightly more complex than was suggested for *hit*, *put* and *set*, and of the same kind, though not wholly automatic. But it should be noted that among the devices used is the idea that one change (or rule) may apply before another – the vowels are shortened before the second consonant is deleted. This 'ordering of rules', too, is commonplace in generative phonology.

So far we have been concerned with changes that take place within words – INTERNAL sandhi. But there are alternations that are found between words where the notion of change may be applied – EXTERNAL sandhi. In English, for example, there is the alternation of *a* and *an*, and of two forms of *the*, /ðə/ and /ðiː/, before consonants and vowels. The apparent addition (or non-deletion) of a consonant is sometimes called 'liaison'; but can we decide whether the *n* of *an* is added or deleted? Another liaison feature in English is that of the so-called 'linking *r*', where in some dialects, including Standard English, an *r* in the spelling is pronounced only before a vowel, but not before a consonant as in:

> *The pore is dirty*   /pɔːr iz/
> *The pore may be dirty*   /pɔː mei/

We may contrast this with a word with no *r* in the spelling:

The paw is dirty.	/pɔ: iz/
The paw may be dirty.	/pɔ: mei/

Here we should wish to say that /r/ is deleted before a consonant. The alternative would be to say that it is added before a vowel, but that would incorrectly predict that both *pore* and *paw* are /pɔ:r/ before a vowel. (In fact, that is the case for some speakers, in which case we cannot decide whether it is added or deleted.) This phenomenon also occurs internally as shown by the contrast of *sawing* and *soaring*.

There is a similar, but more complicated, feature in French (for which the term 'liaison' was first used). As a fairly general rule many word-final consonants are deleted, except before vowels within certain grammatical constructions. This exception applies even to the masculine forms of adjectives, which, as we saw on p. 105, are derivable from feminine forms by the deletion of the final consonant. It is this non-deletion that is called 'liaison'. Without liaison we have masculine and feminine pairs:

le petit garçon	(/pəti/)	'the little boy'
la petite fille	(/pətit/)	'the little girl'

With liaison, however, we find:

le petit homme	(/pətit/)	'the little man'

h here has no phonetic realization; *homme* begins with a vowel and forces liaison. The situation is complicated by the fact that liaison sometimes does not take place (there is deletion) even with words beginning with a vowel. Thus *hibou* 'owl' also begins with a vowel, but there is no liaison:

le petit hibou	(/pəti/)	'the little owl'

Moreover, elision of, for instance, the *e* of the article *le* takes place with *homme*, but not *hibou* – *l'homme*, but *le hibou*. This is dealt with in grammars of French by talking about 'aspirate *h*', a very curious term when French has no [h] at all. What we could suggest is that words like *hibou* begin with a consonant, which prevents both liaison and elision. But we must then say either that this consonant has no phonetic realization, but is like zero, or that it is deleted after it has blocked liaison and elision.

Both may seem a little implausible, but some device is needed to account for the facts.

There is an even more curious liaison feature in Italian. A small number of monosyllabic words such as *da* 'from', *vá* 'it goes' (but not *di* 'of' or *la* 'the') require that the first consonant of the following word be geminated:

> *da Roma*   (/da rró:ma/)   'from Rome'
> *va bene*   (/vá bbéne/)   'all right'

It is easy enough to state what happens informally, but very difficult to put into a formal analysis. A strict IA analysis would entail that every word of Italian beginning with a consonant had two forms, one used after these little words, and the other used elsewhere. As with aspirate *h*, we need to indicate something – perhaps some kind of consonant that assimilates completely with the following consonant. Whatever we do the underlying form will be very artificial in appearance.

Morphological patterns are very complex and varied. In some languages many different processes seem to be taking place and some of the alternations can be explained only formally by quite abstract forms and a complex set of ordered rules. We are often faced with a dilemma. Do we set up these complex analyses and risk implausibility, or do we simply list all the various forms and fail to provide any kind of explanation?

3.3 The morphology of derivation

The discussion so far has been concerned with variation in closely related grammatical forms of words, involving morpho-syntactic categories (pp. 54, 78) such as number, gender, tense and mood. It has necessarily been limited to inflectional languages (or, more strictly, to the inflectional features of languages) because agglutinative languages have, by definition, no variation, while isolating languages have no morphology. It has been concerned, that is to say, solely with inflection, to the exclusion of derivation (pp. 54–5).

Since, however, there are some partial regularities, a study of word-formation (as derivation is often called) is possible. It is perfectly possible to classify in terms of change of word class, shape of the suffixes, meaning relations, etc. Moreover, because there is some regularity in the sound changes, some scholars have dealt with derivation in morphological terms. Indeed, even

Bloomfield handled the relation between *duke* and *duchess* in terms of phonetic modification.

More recently, in generative phonology, an attempt has been made to deal with derivation in almost exactly the same way as inflection. Thus, for Chomsky and Halle a single set of rules will account for all of the following pairs (and others too):

profane	*profanity*
serene	*serenity*
divine	*divinity*

The spelling disguises considerable differences in the vowels of the second syllable:

/prəfein/	/prəfæniti/
/səri:n/	/səreniti/
/divain/	/diviniti/

It will be seen that whereas the words in the first column, the adjectives, have a diphthong or a long vowel, the words in the second, the derived nouns, have a short vowel; moreover, the vowels differ in quality – the /i:/ of *serene* does not change to /i/ in *serenity* but to /e/. To account for this Chomsky and Halle postulate underlying forms:

profǣn   serēn   divīn

To generate the adjectives (the first column) there is first a rule of diphthongization which adds y to give:

profǣyn   serēyn   divīyn

There is a second rule of vowel shift (ǣ to ē, ē to ī and ī to ǣ), to give:

profēyn   serīyn   divǣyn

Some further rules convert these into the correct phonetic forms. For the nouns in the second column there is one rule only, a 'laxing' rule, which effectively simply makes the long vowels (of the underlying forms) short to give:

profænity   serenity   divinity

Again a few minor changes are needed to give the correct phonetic forms (e.g. of y into the vowel /i/).

This analysis may seem rather artificial and contrived, and perhaps to say no more than that /ei/ becomes /æ/, /i:/ becomes

/e/ and /ai/ becomes /i/ when the suffix -*ity* is added to an adjective to form a noun. But there are two points to be made in its favour. First, there are regularities of this kind, even if only partial ones. We may compare *sane/sanity*, *obscene/obscenity*, and in a different type of derivation *oblige/obligation*, as well as the possible /iː/–/e/ variation in the inflection of the verb discussed on p. 116. If there are such regular variations, they ought to be stated. Few scholars before Chomsky and Halle had made any attempt to investigate them (except from a historical point of view). Secondly, these rules are not invented simply for this particular pattern; the aim is to have an overall set of rules that apply to all inflectional and derivational patterns. It must be said that the enormous complexity and variation in the morphophonological patterns of derivation in English would seem to make it impossible to arrive at any wholly plausible integrated analysis, yet that is, in fact, what Chomsky and Halle attempted to do. The details of their analysis have been challenged, and it may be that an overall analysis is not feasible. But there are plenty of interesting and important observations in this work.

4 Sentence Structure

Traditional ideas on syntax, the grammar of sentences (morphology being the grammar of words), have already been discussed, mostly in 2.4. In the last few decades syntax has undoubtedly become the most intensively studied topic within linguistics, and many new ideas and new linguistic models have been put forward, but it must be acknowledged that, even in recent times, most of the best descriptive accounts of actual languages have been written in fairly conservative terms and have only partly been influenced by modern theoretical proposals.

4.1 IC analysis

It is reported that an American linguist of the 1950s remarked that syntax was that part of linguistics that everyone hoped the other fellow would do. For although the structuralists believed that they had largely succeeded in solving the problems of morphology, they realized that they had little to offer towards the analysis of the sentence. They had discovered and defined the morpheme, but still needed to establish what other grammatical units there were and how they were distributed. Their approach to the problem was, characteristically, to divide the sentence up into IMMEDIATE CONSTITUENTS or ICs. For their aim was to discover the relevant linguistic elements, and it was not clear that there were any definable units beyond the morpheme, apart from the sentence. The initial emphasis was, as a result, on simply dividing the sentence into its constituent elements, without knowing, to begin with, what those elements might be. The principle of IC analysis is, then, to cut a sentence into two and then to cut those parts into two and to continue with the segmentation until the smallest indivisible units, the morphemes, are reached. Occasionally it is difficult to divide into two, and, rarely, segmentation into three or more elements may be permitted, but as a general principle the division is binary.

121

This can be illustrated with the sentence *The young man followed a girl*. This can first be divided into *the young man* and *followed a girl*. Then *followed a girl* is divided into *followed* and *a girl*, and *the young man* into *the* and *young man*; the final divisions are between *young* and *man*, and *follow-* and *-ed*. We can show the order of segmentation by using one upright line for the first cut, two for the second, and so on, arriving finally at:

The‖ young‖‖ man| follow‖‖ ed‖ a‖‖ girl

Another, now more common, name for this analysis is BRACKETING: brackets are used, as in algebra. This is more difficult to read unless the brackets are numbered, to show which opening and closing brackets belong together, although it is, in fact, unambiguous (for one should always check to make sure that there is the same number of opening and closing brackets):

((The (((young) (man))) ((followed) ((a) (girl)))

Quite the best method of display is the use of a 'tree', rather like that of a family tree where the 'branching' shows the divisions. The tree diagram for our sentence is:

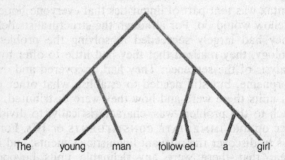

The   young   man   follow ed   a   girl

We would similarly analyse the much more complex sentence *The young man with a paper followed a girl in a blue dress*: The diagram (facing page) brings out very clearly the hierarchical nature of IC analysis: the smallest elements combine to form larger ones and so on 'upwards'.

How do we know where to make the cuts, particularly the first one? The answer lies in the notion of EXPANSION. A sequence of elements is said to be an expansion of another if it can be substituted for it; substitution is a basic procedure in all structuralist analyses.

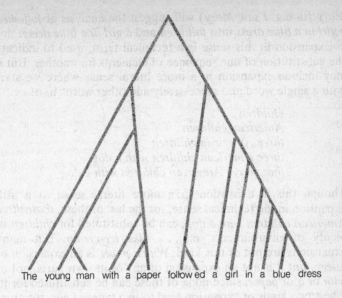

The young man with a paper followed a girl in a blue dress

In the sentence we have just considered the first ICs are *the young man with a paper* and *followed a girl in a blue dress*. But why is this segmentation chosen rather than, say, that of *the young man with a paper followed* and *a girl in a blue dress*? The argument is as follows. First, we can establish that *the young man with a paper* is an expansion of *John*, since *John* can be substituted for it in *John followed a girl in a blue dress*. Similarly, we can establish *followed a girl in a blue dress* as an expansion of, say, *arrived*, since we can say *The young man with a paper arrived*. Then we may compare all of this with *John arrived*; here the obvious ICs are into *John* and *arrived*. On the analogy of this sentence, together with arguments concerning expansion, we can conclude that the ICs of our longer sentence are *the young man with a paper* and *followed a girl in a blue dress*.

Similar procedures allow us to continue further with our analysis. We may compare *the young man with a paper* with *people here*, showing first that *the young man* is an expansion of *people* (*people with a paper*) and then that *with a paper* is an expansion of *here* (*the young man here*); if the ICs of *people here* are *people* and *here*, the ICs of *the young man with a paper* are *the young man* and *with a paper*. By similar procedures *saw*

Mary (in e.g. *I saw Mary*) will suggest the analysis of *followed a girl in a blue dress* into *followed* and *a girl in a blue dress*.

Expansion in this sense is a technical term, used to indicate the substitution of one sequence of elements for another. But it may include expansion in a more literal sense where we start with a single word and successively add other words to it:

> *children*
> *American children*
> *three American children*
> *three American children with a dog*
> *those three American children with a dog*

Though this is expansion in a more literal sense, it is still expansion in the technical sense, for the last of these, *those three American children with a dog*, can be substituted for *children* in plenty of environments, e.g., ... *like ice-cream*. But many expansions are not of this kind. *With a paper* is an expansion of *asleep*, but it is not an expansion of any of its own parts, not of *with* or *a* or *paper*, since none of these can be substituted for it. These two kinds of expansion lead to two types of construction, ENDOCENTRIC and EXOCENTRIC. An endocentric construction is one in which there is expansion of the more literal kind, and thus contains an element, a word, for which it (the whole construction) can be substituted. This word is known as the HEAD; in our example the head is *children*. An exocentric construction cannot be similarly substituted for any of its elements and thus has no head. It is essentially because of endocentricity that we can talk about noun phrases, verb phrases, etc. (see pp. 70–71), for these are endocentric constructions with nouns, verbs, etc. as their heads.

Although segmentation is largely based, in IC analysis, on the substitution possibilities, another criterion (which is consistent with the main tenets of structuralism) is distribution. We shall find, that is to say, that the same constituent occurs in different places in the structure; this too will help us with the identification. For instance, we find that *to go* is an obvious constituent in, say, *to go is fun*. We may, therefore, argue that it is also a constituent in *wants to go* and so analyse *wants to go* into *wants* and *to go* rather than *wants to* and *go*. Similarly, *the King of England* is to be divided into *the* and *King of England* rather than *the King* and *of England* in view of *He became King of England*.

Simply dividing a sentence into ICs does not provide much information. Nevertheless it can sometimes prove illuminating. It can, for instance, show that a certain type of ambiguity, a difference of meaning, is related to a difference in the hierarchical structure of the IC analysis. An often quoted example is *the old men and women*. The ambiguity is clearly illustrated by paraphrasing it as either 'the old men and the women' or 'the old men and the old women'. This would allow us to recognize two different analyses, as shown by the trees:

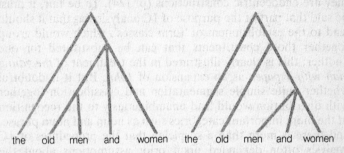

the   old   men   and   women   the   old   men   and   women

(There is a slight complication here in that, with a conjunction such as *and*, it is difficult to provide the justification for a binary cut, since there seems no reason to prefer *men and* and *women* to *men* and *and women*, and it seems that we must cut into three.) Similarly we can disambiguate (resolve the ambiguity of) *Egyptian cotton shirt* by having the first cut after *Egyptian* ('a cotton shirt made in Egypt') or after *cotton* ('a shirt made of Egyptian cotton'). Less obvious is the ambiguity in *He looked over my shoulder*. If this refers to a doctor examining the shoulder, the second cut will be between *looked over* and *my shoulder*, but if it simply refers to the direction in which someone looked, the division will be between *looked* and *over my shoulder*. Much more difficult and, perhaps, not soluble in terms of IC analysis alone (see pp. 146–7), is the problem of *He said he was coming today*. If *today* is taken to 'belong' to *said*, the first cut is, presumably, after *coming*; if it 'belongs' to *coming*, the cut will occur after *said*:

He said he was coming | today.
He said | he was coming today.

However, merely dividing actually occurring sentences out into their constituent parts is unsatisfactory for several reasons.

In the first place, it does not indicate what kind of elements those constituent parts are; it does not even identify, except by implication, any part of one sentence with any part of another. Yet it is obvious that, in the sentence we considered earlier, *man* and *girl* are the same kind of constituent, for both are nouns. It is also the case that *the young man with a paper* is the same kind of constituent as *a girl in a blue dress*; both may be identified as noun phrases. Secondly, it does not show clearly that noun phrases are built on nouns, verb phrases on verbs etc., i.e. that they are endocentric constructions (p. 124). To be fair, it must be said that part of the purpose of IC analysis was that it should lead to the establishment of 'form classes', which would group together those constituents that can be substituted for one another; this is clearly illustrated in the treatment of *the young man with a paper* as an expansion of *John*. But it is doubtful whether quite simple segmentation and classification together with distribution would lead unambiguously to the recognition of the more important categories such as noun and noun phrase, and there is more than a suspicion that the procedures of IC analysis often depended upon prior assumptions about the grammar of the language, and this involved some circularity of argument.

A third point is that IC analysis does not tell us how to form new sentences, i.e. to produce sentences that have not already been attested in some corpus of data. Now it is obvious that the sentence *A girl in a blue dress followed the young man with a paper* is as grammatical a sentence of English as the one we have been discussing, for the very simple reason that *a girl in a blue dress* and *the young man with a paper* are constituents of the same type (noun phrases). Although IC analysis will analyse the sentence correctly if it occurs, it will not predict that it could occur in English, i.e., that it is a possible sentence of the language. This is a matter of the philosophy of structuralism which will be discussed again later (5.6), but is, surely, a curious restriction on what a grammar should do. We need rather to be able to specify, precisely and explicitly, not just sentences that have occurred but also the possible grammatical sentences of a language.

4.2 Phrase structure grammar

What is needed is a model that will not merely segment the constituents, but will also identify them in grammatical terms, and will, in addition, change the emphasis of the linguistic analysis from mere description of sentences that have actually occurred to the specification of what sentences are possible in a language. Such a model is generative; it is said to GENERATE all the grammatical sentences of a language. The model that will be discussed in this section is associated with transformational generative grammar, which is the topic of the next chapter, but since it deals with the constituency structure and not the transformational aspects of that grammar, it is convenient to deal with it here.

One method of IC analysis that was discussed is the use of brackets, or bracketing. The bracketed elements can, however, be given grammatical identification by what is aptly known as LABELLED BRACKETING. Let us consider the sentence *The man followed a girl*. In this sentence *the* and *a* can be identified as determiners, *man* and *girl* as nouns and *followed* as a verb (this can, of course, be analysed further as *follow-* and *-ed*, or as the past tense of FOLLOW, but this is not wholly relevant here and will be ignored). Moreover, *the man* and *a girl* are also constituents of the same, but larger, type, noun phrases, and if our IC analysis is correct *followed a girl* is also a constituent, a verb phrase, while the whole is a sentence or clause. With the use of the symbols DET for 'determiner', N for 'noun', V for 'verb', NP for 'noun phrase', VP for 'verb phrase' and S for 'sentence', a labelled bracketing of the sentence can be provided:

$$[_S [_{NP} [_{DET} \text{ the}] [_N \text{ man}]] [_{VP} [_V \text{ followed}] [_{NP} [_{DET} \text{ a}] [_N \text{ girl}]]]]$$

The symbols, the 'labels', are attached in subscript form to one of each pair of brackets; it is now the convention to attach them to the first, the left hand, bracket, and to use square brackets. The same analysis, the phrase structure of the sentence, can be displayed in a tree diagram, which again is easier to read than the system of brackets (see p. 128). The representation of the phrase structure of a sentence is known as its PHRASE MARKER or P-MARKER for short. The points that are joined by the lines or 'branches' are called NODES. Each of the nodes, except those on the bottom line (which are the TERMINAL nodes), is given a label that represents a grammatically definable constituent – N,

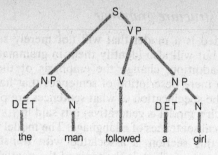

V, NP, VP, etc. Where one node is higher in the tree than
another and joined to it by branches, it is said to DOMINATE it;
if it is placed immediately above it and joined by a single line, it
IMMEDIATELY dominates it. DOMINANCE, thus, shows how a
larger constituent may consist of one or more constituents of a
smaller kind (but see 4.4 for possible exceptions to this). It is
important to notice that the tree structure preserves the linear
order of the constituents, just as plain IC analysis does. The first
noun phrase precedes the verb phrase, the verb precedes the
second noun phrase, the determiner precedes the noun. PRE-
CEDENCE, thus, like dominance is clearly shown in the tree
diagram.

Labelled bracketing and phrase structure trees provide much
more information than IC analysis, but they still do not state,
except by implication, how new sentences can be generated. This
can be done with the use of PHRASE STRUCTURE RULES (PS-
RULES). The tree structure and labelled bracketing that we have
been considering can be generated by six rules:

(1) S → NP – VP
(2) VP → V – NP
(3) NP → DET – N
(4) V → followed
(5) DET → the, a
(6) N → man, girl

These rules are not difficult to interpret. The first says that a
sentence (S) can consist of (or be expanded into or be formed
from) a noun phrase (NP) and a verb phrase (VP) in that
sequence, and the second that a verb phrase (VP) can consist of
a verb (V) and a following noun phrase (NP), and so on. These
rules provide all the information given in the tree diagram. The

first rule, for instance, is matched in the diagram by the S node immediately dominating NP and VP and the second by the VP node dominating V and NP.

These rules are, of course, quite different from the rules of traditional grammar that were discussed in 1.3. Those were essentially prescriptive or normative, telling us how we ought to speak and write, saying that, for instance, we ought not to end a sentence with a preposition, or say *It's me*. Most such rules have no validity and little relevance to a linguistic analysis of the sentence, beyond the fact that they have become accepted by many people as a kind of faith, for their origins lie in false analogy with Latin, in pseudo-logic or in pure invention. The rules we are now discussing are, or should be, descriptive, telling us something about the actual principles of grammar and the facts of language. Their justification lies solely in the function they perform in allowing us to talk systematically about language structure and not in any preconceived notions of what is correct or incorrect.

These rules will not generate only the one sentence handled in the tree diagram – *The man followed a girl*. For since both *the* and *a* are shown as determiners and both *man* and *girl* as nouns, the rules permit us to permute the determiners in each determiner position and the two nouns in each noun position and, in fact, to generate no less than sixteen different sentences including, for instance:

> *A girl followed the man.*
> *The girl followed a man.*
> *A man followed a man.*

etc.

In a similar manner phrase structure rules for our longer sentence would generate not only *The young man with a paper followed a girl in a blue dress*, but equally *A girl in a blue dress followed the young man with a paper*, if both *the young man with a paper* and *a girl in a blue dress* are noun phrases.

Even if we restrict our attention to rules like 1–3, we shall need many other rules. Since English, like many other languages, has intransitive verbs, verbs that do not require an object (see p. 71), it clearly follows that VP is not always expanded into V – NP, but may be expanded into V alone. An example, with the appropriate rule, is:

The man smiled.
(VP→V)

Instead of writing two different rules for the expansion of VP, we can write a single rule to show that the presence of an NP is 'optional', by enclosing it in round brackets:

VP→V (– NP)

This says that a VP may be expanded into V with or without a following NP.

There are, however, many other expansions of VP, as was, in fact, first suggested in the examples on p. 74. Some of those examples may be given again with the appropriate rules (using A for 'adjective' and PP for 'prepositional phrase'):

John seems happy	(VP→V – A)
The boy sat on the floor.	(VP→V – PP)
The girl made John happy.	(VP→V – NP – A)
I gave the man a book.	(VP→V – NP – NP)

These different structures are, of course, closely associated with the lexical verbs that are used. This is the reason that traditional grammar distinguishes between transitive and intransitive verbs – for we cannot say (asterisks again indicating impossible sentences):

*The woman hit.
*The man smiled the book.

Similarly, the other constructions are restricted in terms of the verb, since we cannot say:

*John seems on the table.
*The book is John happy.
*The girl made happy.
*I gave happy on the table.

We can collapse all the rules into one:

$$VP\rightarrow V \begin{pmatrix} (-NP) & \begin{matrix} (-NP) \\ (-A) \end{matrix} \\ -PP \end{pmatrix}$$

But this will do no more than summarize all the possible constituents of a VP. It will not imply that any, or all of them, will occur with a particular verb. The problem of the way in which sentence structures are associated with particular lexical verbs is discussed in 4.3.

There is, however, a very different sense in which elements are 'optional'. Prepositional phrases will occur with most verbs in addition to the elements indicated in the rules above and so can be added almost freely to any sentence. (There are a few possible restrictions.) Even more obviously, attributive adjectives freely occur before nouns. We find both *the boys* and *the little boys*, showing the need for a rule:

$$NP \rightarrow DET\ (-A) - NP$$

Indeed we shall even need to suggest that several adjectives may occur in this position as in *the naughty little English boys*. The issue of 'purely' optional elements such as the attributive adjectives is dealt with in 4.4.

It was suggested in 4.1 that one possible test of constituency was that of distribution, that, for instance, we might analyse *wants to go* into *wants* and *to go*, because *to go* is found as a constituent in *To go is fun*. That is, however, to recognize that these constituents have grammatical functions that are not restricted to the narrow confines of expansion, and it is reasonable, therefore, to look for other, more general, indications of constituency. We will briefly discuss three that have been suggested.

First, it is said that only constituents may be coordinated with conjunctions such as *and*. Thus we may say:

> *The young man followed the girl and the child.*
> *The young man followed the girl and spoke to her.*

In the first *the girl* and *the child* (both NPs) are coordinated, while in the second *followed the girl* and *spoke to her* are coordinated, both being VPs. But we cannot say:

> **The young man followed the girl and woman followed the man.*

Man followed the girl and *woman followed the man* are alike in structure but they are not constituents, as can be seen from our previous analyses, and cannot, therefore, be coordinated.

This test allows us to recognize different constituency in:

> *He ran down the hill.*
> *He ran down the company*

For whereas we can say

> *He ran down the hill and down the valley,*

we cannot say

> **He ran down the company and down its organization.*

In the first example the constituency of the VP is *ran* and *down the hill*; in the second it is *ran down* and *the company*. We can, therefore, say

> *He ran down the company and its organization.*

We can, of course, also say

> *He ran down the hill and the valley.*

For although *down the hill* is a constituent, it has the further constituency *down* and *the hill* – *the hill* is also a constituent. However, this test will not always work. Consider the sentence:

> *Switzerland has extremely high mountains and deep valleys.*

The most natural interpretation is in terms of 'extremely deep valleys', i.e. that *extremely* modifies both *high mountains* and *deep valleys*, which are coordinated. But *high mountains* is not a constituent in *extremely high mountains*. The ICs are *extremely high* (an adjectival phrase) and *mountains*.

A second possible criterion is that only constituents may act as the antecedents of certain pronouns. Most commonly, NPs act as the antecedents of pronouns, as in:

> *I saw the old woman and spoke to her.*

Yet pronouns seem to have sentences also as their antecedents as in:

> A. *Mary is coming tomorrow.*   B. *I don't believe it.*
> *John said Mary is coming tomorrow, but I don't believe it.*

There are, however, problems, and it could be argued that such sentences are essentially NPs; traditional grammars speak of 'noun clauses'. (This will be discussed in 4.4.) In any case, the pronoun test will establish only one, or possibly two, types of constituent, and will tell us nothing of the other types.

Thirdly, it has been argued that only constituents may be omitted as in:

> *John will see the man, but Mary won't.*

This suggests that *see the man* is a constituent. If this is so, the modal verb *will* does not form a constituent with the rest of the verbal elements, and the constituency of the verb phrase is not *will see* and *the man*. The suggested tree structure is:

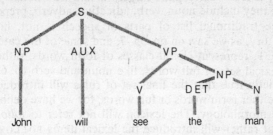

This is contrary to the traditional view, and indeed the common-sense one, that the auxiliary verb is a modifier of the main verb. Moreover, if putative constituents of this type can be omitted, it is difficult to explain why we cannot say:

> *John doesn't want to see the man, but Mary wants,*

or *John didn't keep talking, but Mary kept.*

What we find here, of course, is the auxiliary DO – ... *but Mary does,* ... *but Mary did,* which suggests very strongly that we are concerned here not with issues of constituency but with the highly specialized functions of auxiliary verbs in English, one of which is, as H. E. Palmer put it, 'avoidance of repetition', a very idiosyncratic kind of proformation in which all auxiliary verbs can function as 'pro-verbs'.

4.3 The lexicon

There is an important difference between the first three and the last three PS rules that were presented on p. 128. The first three all expanded grammatical categories into other grammatical categories, S into NP – VP, VP into V – NP, NP into DET – N; all the additional rules discussed in the last section were of the same type. They belong exclusively to the grammar and are known as CATEGORIAL RULES. The last three rules, by contrast, expanded grammatical categories into words of the language, V into *followed*, DET into *the* or *a*, N into *man* or *girl*; these lead directly to the terminal nodes, and so to the output of the rules, which will be an English sentence. Most of the information provided by these rules is to be found in the dictionary or lexicon, for the dictionary will tell us that MAN and GIRL are nouns, that FOLLOW is a verb.

The categories that are replaced in the rules by lexical items – N, V, DET – correspond largely to the traditional parts of speech; they include noun, verb, adjective, adverb, preposition, etc. The traditional list of parts of speech is not, however, satisfactory, as we saw on pp. 55–7, and some of the categories, e.g. DET, represent closed classes of form words, rather than open lexical sets of full words, like noun and verb (p. 60). Nor is it strictly true that the final set of rules will introduce only words, either form words or full words, for we have deliberately ignored morphology. The lexicon will not refer to *followed* or *man*, but rather will introduce the lexical items FOLLOW (with past tense form *followed*) and MAN (with singular *man* but plural *men*). We need, therefore, extra rules to deal with morphology, to introduce, for instance, the past tense ending *-ed* after *follow*. Chomsky distinguished between lexical FORMATIVES such as *follow* and grammatical formatives such as *-ed* (or *-ing* or the *-s* of singular verbs and plural nouns). It is these that will be introduced by the final set of rules, though we shall also have rather more complex statements (of the kind discussed in Chapter 3) to deal with *took* or *men*. But the final set of rules, which introduces the terminal nodes, must expand the categories into formatives of this kind if we are to generate grammatical sentences of English.

In addition to specifying which words are nouns, verbs, etc., there are two other kinds of information that the lexicon should provide. First, it must indicate which of the various expansions of VP are associated with the different lexical verbs. It is for this reason that a dictionary will describe a verb as 'transitive' or 'intransitive', to determine whether, for that verb, the VP can be expanded into V – NP or not. But the lexicon ought also to distinguish such verbs as SEEM where the VP may be expanded into V – A, or SIT where the expansion is V – PP, or PUT with V – NP – PP. This can be achieved by clearly indicating for each verb what are the structures into which it may be inserted by lexical insertion rules. We need to state that SEEM, but not SIT may occur before an adjective, and that HIT must be followed by a noun phrase, but that SMILE cannot be. The rules needed for this are called SUBCATEGORIZATION RULES, for they designate subcategories of the major lexical categories in terms of these characteristics. Thus we might have entries such as:

> follow: V, + [—— NP]
> smile: V, − [—— NP]

These say that FOLLOW and SMILE are both verbs (V), and that FOLLOW occurs in the environment of a following NP, while SMILE does not. (The position into which a lexical item may be inserted is shown by the long dash, while the plus and minus signs indicate whether such insertion is possible or not.) We shall then need to add:

> seem: V, + [—— A]
> sit: V, + [—— PP]

These rules are not sufficient as they stand, however, because we also need to indicate that verbs like SMILE and SIT do not occur with a following NP. But if we are to indicate not only the environments in which a verb occurs but also all the environments in which it does not, we shall need a very long lexical entry for each, referring to all possible environments. For simplicity, therefore, it is usual to omit all the negative specifications and to state only the positive ones, with the convention that if the subcategorization does not positively state that an element may occur in a given structure, it is to be assumed that it cannot. We shall not, then, need for SMILE the rule that it does not occur before an NP.

The rules will be quite detailed and complex. For PUT we need to indicate that it occurs with NP – PP (e.g. *He put the book on the table.*):

> put: V, + [—— NP – PP]

The same rule might seem to apply to ACCUSE in view of:

> *He accused the man of treachery.*

Yet there is a further restriction here in that with this verb, the only possible preposition is *of*; we can therefore actually specify *of* in the rule:

> accuse: V, + [—— NP of NP]

In fact, there are restrictions on the preposition with PUT too; it may be *in, on, out, under, over*, but not *for* or *to* (except in the idiomatic *put something to someone*). All the prepositions that may be used indicate place or location, and so may be described as 'locative'. We can, therefore, add this information too by indicating that the PP must be locative.

Many verbs will be subcategorized for more than one structure. MAKE, for instance, is associated with at least three:

> I made a model.
> I made the boy happy.
> I made the boy their leader.

We need to specify all of these:

make: V, + [—— NP], + [—— NP – A], + [—— NP – NP]

We can, however, collapse these three structures into one if we use round brackets to indicate optional elements:

$$\text{make: V, } + [\text{—— NP} \begin{pmatrix} -\text{ A} \\ -\text{ NP} \end{pmatrix}]$$

In a similar way we can show that EAT is either intransitive or transitive (*I have already eaten*, *I have eaten my lunch*):

eat: V, + [—— (NP)]

So far only the subcategorization of verbs has been discussed. But other categories may be analysed in the same way. Adjectives, for instance, have restrictions on the prepositions that may occur with them – *sure of*, *eager for*, *content with*, *opposed to* and (for the more pedantic of us) *different from*. These can equally be shown by such entries as:

sure: A, + [—— of NP]
eager: A, + [—— for NP]

Subcategorization rules are also needed for nouns, to deal with the distinction between countables and uncountables and so ensure that we say *There is a book* ... but *There is butter* ... (see p. 58). Similarly subcategorization of nouns will be required to account for gender in a language such as French.

A second and different kind of restriction is to be found in the observation that we should not normally say:

> *He drank the bread.
> *Sincerity admires John.

Clearly this, too, is a matter to be handled in the lexicon. We need to specify that DRINK will occur with nouns that denote liquids and that verbs such as ADMIRE need animate subjects.

We can achieve this, too, with entries rather like those already discussed:

> drink: V, + [——— NP + liquid]
> admire: V, + [NP + animate ———]

But these restrictions are different from those dealt with by subcategorization, for they restrict lexical items in terms of other lexical items and not in terms of grammatical structures involving grammatical categories. Nevertheless they are important, as can be seen if we reconsider the sentence discussed in 4.2 – *The young man with a paper followed a girl in a blue dress*. If our rules show that *man*, *paper*, *girl* and *dress* are all nouns with no restrictions, there is nothing to prevent the generation of a large number of quite impossible sentences such as:

   The blue girl with a man followed a paper in a young dress.

The restrictions that are required to rule out such sentences as these are known as SELECTIONAL RESTRICTIONS. In an early form of transformational generative grammar it was thought that they, too, should be treated, like the subcategorization rules, as part of the syntax. But they are not rules in quite the same sense. For let us consider again *John drank the bread*. If confronted with this we should probably not say that it is incorrect or ungrammatical, but try to make sense of it by saying either that *bread* must be the name of something that people can drink (perhaps a slang expression) or that it was bread that had been liquidized. But we cannot make sense of sentences in the same way that breach subcategorization rules. Faced with

   John seemed in the chair.
   He smiled the man.

we shall simply say that these are ungrammatical and probably amend them to *John seemed to be in the chair*, *He smiled at the man*. Where selectional restrictions are involved we can always try to find a context or reinterpret the lexical items in some way. We can even, if we try hard enough, make sense of what at first seems complete nonsense. For instance, it has been claimed that with sufficient ingenuity one can contextualize Chomsky's famous example:

   Colourless green ideas sleep furiously.

What is at issue with selectional restrictions is not grammar so much as semantics or meaning. Given a verb like DRINK we expect that the following noun will denote something liquid. If we do not know the word we shall assume that it is liquid. For instance, hearing *The children drank the zoom*, we may well believe that 'zoom' is the name of a new fizzy drink. For reasons of this kind selectional restrictions should not be treated as part of the syntax at all. They are not formal, but to a large degree semantic, and the place for stating meanings of lexical items is not in the grammar but in the lexicon. However, although selectional restrictions are basically semantic, they are not necessarily universal, the same for all languages. In English we can use EAT as well as DRINK with SOUP (*He ate all his soup*), but it is unlikely that a similar statement can be made for many other languages. Conversely, the word for 'drink' in Arabic is also used with the word for 'cigarette'. Arabic speakers do not 'smoke' cigarettes, they 'drink' them. It is because selectional restrictions are in many respects specific to individual languages in spite of their semantic basis, that literal translations are so very comic.

4.4 Further issues

We now turn to consider two issues that were not dealt with in the original proposal for phrase structure grammars and also two that raise problems for any form of constituency analysis.

The first problem concerns the constituency of endocentric constructions. We saw earlier (p. 126) that IC analysis does not explicitly show the centrality of N to NP, of V to VP, etc. It can also be argued that PS rules fail to do this. Furthermore we may not have enough labels to distinguish the various kinds of constituents that we need to recognize. This arises in the constituency analysis of *the little boys*. The whole is a noun phrase, *boys* is a noun, but what is the status of *little boys*? There is no doubt that it is a constituent and that the PS structure of the phrase is:

$$[_{NP} [_{DET} the] [_? [_A little] [_N boys]]]$$

The fact that *little boys* is a constituent is clear enough from substitution procedures in IC analysis, and is confirmed by the test of coordination. For consider:

> *The little boys and the big girls*
> *The little boys and big girls*
> *The little boys and girls*

In the first *the little boys* and *the big girls*, both NPs, are coordinated. In the third *boys* and *girls*, both Ns, are coordinated. But in the second the constituents that are coordinated are *little boys* and *big girls*. The test shows, therefore, that *little boys* is a constituent of another kind.

Although we have the labels NP for *the little boys* and N for *boys*, we have no label for *little boys*. We need, moreover, to show that it too is some kind of nominal element. Indeed this is implicit in the description of *the little boys* as an endocentric construction (see p. 124). Instead, however, of simply inventing another name for this intermediate constituent, a device known as 'X-bar syntax' has been proposed. The idea is that if we take such a category as N we may indicate the next larger constituent with a bar over the N ($\bar{N}$) and the next larger again with two bars ($\bar{\bar{N}}$) and so on; these can be referred to as 'N bar' and 'N double bar', etc. We can now say that *boys* is N, *little boys* $\bar{N}$ and *the little boys* $\bar{\bar{N}}$ (instead of NP).

However, there is no clear limit to the number of words that may be included in a noun phrase; we may simply add adjectives and so produce *the naughty little English boys* or *a tall dark handsome stranger*. Since the constituency of the first of these involves, in succession *boys*, *English boys*, *little English boys* and *naughty little English boys*, it might be supposed that the NP here is to be reanalysed as an N with five bars. But this would be unhelpful for the syntax. For we need to recognize constituents of the same type, and it follows from that that all the structures that were originally considered to be NPs must all now have the same number of bars. For we still need a rule to match our first PS-rule S→NP – VP. Let us assume then that it was right to treat *the little boys* as $\bar{\bar{N}}$ and *little boys* as $\bar{N}$, and that adding further adjectives will not affect the status of the constituent, so that *the naughty little English boys* is also $\bar{\bar{N}}$ and *naughty little English boys* is $\bar{N}$ (see below, p. 142).

However, it is not only expressions like *the little boys* and *the naughty little English boys* that function as NPs and, so, as $\bar{\bar{N}}$s in our revised analysis. *Boys* and *little boys* can have exactly the same status as in:

The little boys fight.
Little boys fight.
Boys fight.

The NP of our original rule must be expandable into all three of these, and we are thus compelled to say that *boys* in the third sentence, is an NP, or $\bar{\bar{N}}$. An $\bar{\bar{N}}$ must, then, consist of at least a noun (or a pronoun) but may also have one or more adjectives and a determiner. We might have the rules:

$$\bar{\bar{N}} \rightarrow (DET)\, \bar{N}$$
$$\bar{N} \rightarrow (A)\, N$$

(But the adjective is optional in a way that the determiner is not – the latter being partly dependent on subcategorization, see p. 134). There is nothing strange, however, about saying that *boys* is $\bar{\bar{N}}$ in our third sentence and N in the first (where *the little boys* is $\bar{\bar{N}}$). But it will follow that if the rules say that $\bar{N}$ may or may not have A, and $\bar{\bar{N}}$ may or may not have both (or either) DET or A, *boys* in the third sentence is not only $\bar{\bar{N}}$ but also $\bar{N}$ and $\underline{N}$. The point becomes clearer if we draw tree structures of the $\bar{\bar{N}}$s (NPs) of the three sentences above:

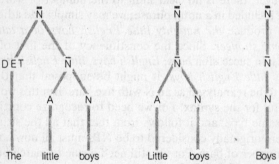

The coordination test shows that all three are $\bar{\bar{N}}$s (*the big girls* is clearly $\bar{\bar{N}}$):

>*The little boys and the big girls*
>*Little boys and the big girls*
>*Boys and the big girls*

The same test shows that *little boys* and *boys* are both $\bar{N}$s (*big girls* being $\bar{N}$):

> *little boys and big girls*
> *boys and big girls*

We have assumed so far that we need only three kinds of constituent distinguished by bars, $\bar{\bar{N}}$, $\bar{N}$ and N. It could be argued that we need four since the presence of a numeral such as *three* in *the three little boys* requires a further distinction; if *three little boys* is $\bar{\bar{N}}$, not $\bar{N}$ (as *little boys* is), *the three little boys* must be N treble bar. We could argue further that *the three little boys in the garden* represents yet a further complication requiring us to have Ns with four bars (and so five different types of constituent in all).

There is no simple proof one way or the other. We can only try to find distributional and general syntactic features to justify the recognition of such different constituents. One argument that has been put forward for $\bar{N}$ is that of proformation. It will be remembered that pronouns have NPs (i.e. $\bar{\bar{N}}$s) as antecedents (p. 59). Where they appear to have single nouns as in *Boys fight whenever they meet*, it is only because those nouns are functioning as $\bar{\bar{N}}$s. But the proform *one* seems often to allow both $\bar{\bar{N}}$s and $\bar{N}$s as its antecedent, as shown by:

> *He has a big red car and I have one too.*
> *He has a big red car and I have a little one.*

In the second sentence the most obvious interpretation is 'a little red car', *one* having the $\bar{N}$ *red car* as its antecedent. There is a slight difficulty in that we might also then expect:

> **He has a big car and I have a one too*.

Here *one* should, we might suppose, have *big car* as its antecedent. But the reason that this does not occur is, presumably, that, since *one* can have $\bar{\bar{N}}$ as its antecedent, . . . *I have one too* is available and preferred.

X-bar syntax does not apply only to noun-like structures. A similar distinction can be made for adjectives in that *very sad* might be $\bar{A}$, if *sad* is A. Similar proposals have been made for V and even for S. But these are complex and some of them depend not on fairly simple arguments like those for N, but on very technical, detailed and specific requirements of the model, and they cannot be simply presented here.

A second problem concerns what is known as RECURSION. We have already made some use of this notion. It was recognized that adjectives may be placed before nouns with apparently no clear limit on the possible number. To account for this fact we simply had a rule that showed the adjective A as optional before the noun N. But, if in *the naughty little English boys* we want to say that the whole phrase is ɪ., and that *boys* is N, we shall also need to say that *English boys*, *little English boys* and *naughty little English boys* are all $\bar{\text{N}}$. Adding an adjective to $\bar{\text{N}}$, that is to say, produces yet another $\bar{\text{N}}$. The rule for this has to be:

$$\bar{\text{N}} \rightarrow (\text{A})\,\bar{\text{N}}$$

This single rule allows any number of adjectives to be added. For once one is added to the $\bar{\text{N}}$ *English boys*, the result *little English boys* is also an $\bar{\text{N}}$, and the rule permits another adjective to be added to it, and so, in theory though not in practice, *ad infinitum*.

There is a very similar situation with coordination, for there is, again, no theoretical limit. We can say *cats and dogs* or *cats, dogs and horses* or *cats, dogs, cows and horses*, etc. Moreover, each time that we coordinate constituents, the result is a constituent of the same kind as the coordinated constituents themselves. $\bar{\bar{\text{N}}}$ *and* $\bar{\bar{\text{N}}}$ is $\bar{\bar{\text{N}}}$, $\bar{\text{N}}$ *and* $\bar{\text{N}}$ is $\bar{\text{N}}$, N *and* N is N. This is clear enough from the examples on p. 139. For the syntactic functions of *the little boys and the big girls* are exactly the same as those of *the little boys*. Both are clearly NP or $\bar{\bar{\text{N}}}$, and the same arguments apply to *little boys and big girls*, which is $\bar{\text{N}}$ just like *little boys* alone, and to *boys and girls*, which is N. Coordination is, in fact, a very general feature that is applicable to adjectives, adverbs, prepositions and even sentences; and, in general, the position is the same: the larger constituent that contains the coordinated constituents has the same status, both in terms of its category and in the number of bars, as the constituents that are coordinated.

This analysis shows up clearly, this time with labels, the ambiguity of *the old men and women*. For the ambiguity rests upon the question whether *women* is $\bar{\text{N}}$ and coordinated with *old men*, or N and so coordinated with *men*. For the coordination of $\bar{\text{N}}$s the tree diagram is the first of the two on the facing page. If the Ns are coordinated (with the meaning 'old men and old women') the diagram is the second.

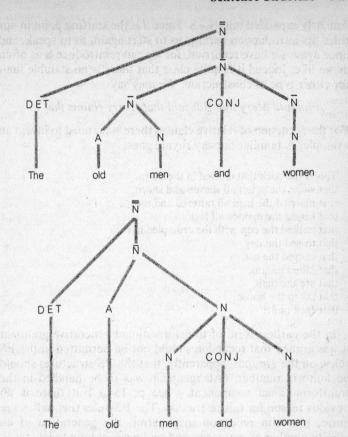

We have considered, then, two kinds of recursion. Rather more fundamental, perhaps, is the recursion that is involved in subordination, or embedding, which was first discussed on p. 72. It was suggested there that in *He said he was coming, he was coming* is not only part of the sentence, but also a sentence (or clause) in its own right, and that the same is true of *who was standing there* in *The little boy who was standing there ran away*. This can be handled in the rules, provided we allow them to introduce sentences or clauses (S). Thus, for our first example, we need to recognize that sentences or clauses can be the complements of verbs, i.e. that VP can be expanded into V – S; in the second *who was standing there* is essentially a modifier of the noun and we need, therefore, to allow that N̄ may be similarly expanded into N – S. Since S is the starting point in our rules, its introduction permits us to start again, so to speak, and once again we have recursion, for we can reintroduce S as often as we like. Indeed it is quite clear that there is no statable limit for either type of construction. We may say:

John told Mary that Bill said that Harry claims that . . .

For the recursion of relative clauses there is no need to invent an example. A familiar nursery rhyme goes:

This is the cock that crowed in the morn,
that woke the priest all shaven and shorn,
that married the man all tattered and torn,
that kissed the maiden all forlorn,
that milked the cow with the crumpled horn,
that tossed the dog,
that chased the cat,
that killed the rat,
that ate the malt,
that lay in the house,
that Jack built.

In the earliest form of transformational generative grammar it was argued that recursion should not be permitted in the PS rules, on the grounds, apparently, that the PS structures should be finite in number. (All recursion was to be handled in the transformational component – see p. 154.) But there is no obvious reason for this restriction. The PS-rules themselves are finite, but with recursion they permit the generation of an infinite number of sentences, and sentences of infinite length. In practice, of course, we do not require this, but we cannot set any theoretical limit on either the number or the length of the sentences for a language and for that reason we cannot establish a complete, but finite, set of possible structures.

There are, naturally, a number of questions to be asked about these structures. Traditional grammar treats *that*-clauses as nominal and relative clauses as adjectival. We could incorporate this into the grammar by treating *that*-clauses as NPs, with a subsequent rule expanding them into S, and similarly we could treat relative clauses as adjectival phrases (or $\overline{A}$ or $\overline{\overline{A}}$). The first of these proposals runs into some difficulty when we analyse sentences with verbs such as HOPE, as is seen when they are compared with sentences with BELIEVE:

> *I hope that he's coming.*
> *I believe that he's coming.*
> **I hope it.* (But: *I hope so.*)
> *I believe it.*
> **I hope his story.*
> *I believe his story.*

There is, clearly, some doubt about the suggestion that the S following HOPE is an NP, for HOPE does not usually have noun phrases as its object (and *so* looks rather like a proform for S, and not NP). The argument for BELIEVE is plausible enough; arguments for NPs with verbs like REGRET are even stronger, since we can say *I regret that . . .* or

> *I regret his action/his having done that,*

but not

> **I believe his action/his having done that.*

There is no simple answer; some embedded Ss are more noun-like than others.

A third problem was discussed in the earliest work on IC analysis. It was tacitly assumed that the ICs will usually be in terms of words, or at least that there will be no division into pieces smaller than words (morphemes) until all the words have been divided. This is clear from the fact that the longer sentences are regarded as expansions of two word sentences such as *John worked*. No one challenges the cut here as *John / worked* because that is the only division if we divide first into words. But there are occasions where dividing first into words or groups of words will not work. There is a notorious example – *the King of England's hat*. Granted that *King of England's* is a constituent (after cutting first between *England's* and *hat* and then between *the* and *King*) how do we now proceed? One might suggest *King / of England's* but surely *King of England's* is like *John's* where the cut must be *John / 's*. So here we must allow for *King of England / 's*. But this is a little strange; one constituent consists of three words plus part of a word, the other of just part of a word.

A simple solution to this problem is to deny that the word has any fundamental place in constituency analysis, and this seems to be generally agreed in work on PS grammars, where the issue is not even raised. Yet this is a little curious, for many of the distributional arguments concern words or sequences of words and it is the fact that words can be isolated that makes them important elements in grammatical units. In some ways they clearly are the most easily recognizable constituents; it is curious, then, if they must sometimes be denied constituent status.

A fourth and much more serious problem is that a linguistic structure often cannot be cut into two because elements that belong together are separated in the sequence. This phenomenon is known as 'discontinuity'. For instance, if we consider *the best team in the world*, it is fairly obvious that *best* and *in the world* belong closely together and that the ICs (ignoring for this purpose the article *the*) are *team* and *best in the world*. But we cannot make a single cut to indicate this because one IC is already in two parts that are separated by the other. A very familiar type of *discontinuity* is provided by the so-called phrasal verbs, MAKE UP, PUT DOWN, TAKE IN, etc., in for example:

> She made the whole story up.
> The conjurer completely took the children in.
> The general soon put the rebellion down.

With such verbs the adverb *up*, *in*, *down*, etc. may often follow the object, as in these examples, yet it clearly belongs with the verb as a single constituent. To take the first example we can first cut into *She* and *made the whole story up*, but what then? The only plausible solution is to recognize a division between *made . . . up* and *the whole story*. There are plenty of other examples of discontinuity; another is *such a lovely house* where presumably we must divide into *a* and *such . . . lovely house*. One of the most important examples is provided by the question forms of the type *Will John come?* Here we must divide into *Will . . . come* and *John*. We cannot possibly show these as ICs by using brackets or the upright lines. We can, if we wish, illustrate by using the tree diagram, but only if we allow the branches to cross one another:

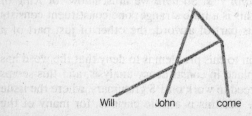

Will   John   come

This is, however, quite unacceptable either for IC analysis or for PS grammars. For IC analysis it simply destroys its whole basis – the assumption that language is essentially a one-dimensional linear string which can be chopped up into decreasing segments. It must be recalled that IC analysis depends on expansion, the substitution of sequences of morphemes by other sequences and by single morphemes, but discontinuous elements are not sequences. PS grammars are more sophisticated, but they, too, cannot deal with discontinuity; the rules (as stated) cannot be interpreted to relate to trees with crossing branches. Each node lies directly beneath the node which dominates it and precedence (sequence) is preserved. An element cannot, then, precede another at any place in the structure if it is dominated by a node that is preceded by a node that dominates the other.

It is often the case that sequences with discontinuous elements have counterparts where the same elements are continuous. We may compare with our previous examples:

> *She made up the whole story.*
> *The conjurer completely took in the children.*
> *The general soon put down the rebellion.*

Even the question form has a parallel statement where there is no discontinuity:

> *John will come.*

This is not, of course, always so. We cannot say:

> **a such lovely house*
> **the best in the world team*

Yet there are sufficient examples of the first type to make it plausible to suggest that the sequence without discontinuity is the more basic and that discontinuity has arisen only because an element has been moved elsewhere, e.g. to the end of the sentence with *up*, *in* and *down*, in *make up*, *took in* and *put down*. Even where there are no parallel constructions we might treat the non-discontinuous asterisked forms as basic, though at an abstract level. This idea of movement is fundamental to the proposals of transformational grammar, as we shall see in the next chapter. Before turning to the proposals in that chapter, however, it may be appropriate to notice that constituency analysis may not always appear to be a sufficient basis for grammatical analysis. One example that has been often quoted is:

> *Flying planes can be dangerous.*

That this may be ambiguous is suggested by the contrast between:

> *Flying planes are dangerous.*
> *Flying planes is dangerous.*

IC analysis will not bring out the ambiguity, as it did in the example *old men and women*, since we can only divide into *flying* and *planes*. Labelled bracketing may go further and even show that in one case *planes* is the head noun and in the other *flying* is the head. But even that will not show that, in a sense, *planes* is the subject of *fly* in the first and its object in the second. We need much more sophisticated syntactic, or perhaps semantic, analysis to make that point clear. Even more difficult is:

> *John is eager to please.*
> *John is easy to please.*

For IC analysis and PS grammars these are identical, even in the labelling of the constituents. Yet we surely want to say that *John* is the subject of *please* in the first and its object in the second. How this can be done is still a matter of controversy, but some solutions will be discussed in Chapter 5.

5 Transformational Generative Grammar

We now turn to consider transformational generative grammar, or TG for short, the theory largely originated and developed by Noam Chomsky. It is without question the most influential theory of linguistics in modern times, and one that no serious scholar can afford to neglect. But the student of TG will often experience frustration and puzzlement, for it is a curious mixture of quite brilliant insights and of complex, technical but often seemingly artificial devices. The primary literature, apart from Chomsky's *Syntactic Structures*, the first published work, is often difficult to read and its full intelligibility depends on knowing all the background.

The notion of PS grammar was discussed in the last chapter and, although much of what was said there comes from Chomsky's works, it is not upon his proposals concerning this that his fame rests. Much more important is the notion of transformation, together with ideas that are associated with it, or have developed out of a transformationally based theory. Although *Syntactic Structures*, published in 1957, first introduced the world to this important theory, *The Logical Structure of Linguistic Theory*, which was not published until eighteen years later, was written some years before it. The theory was, undoubtedly, revolutionary and even greeted with total scepticism by many scholars, but, as with all revolutions, some of it had been foreshadowed in earlier works, particularly in the writings of Chomsky's own teacher Zellig Harris, and there had already been some movement away from the rather rigid and sterile attitudes of the post-Bloomfieldian structuralists.

Chomsky has considerably modified his ideas since 1957, and in his philosophical views has vastly distanced himself from the structuralists, and indeed from the whole of the empiricist tradition (see pp. 100, 193). Undoubtedly the best known, in some ways neatest and most discussed theoretical position is that of

Aspects of the Theory of Syntax, a position that Chomsky himself has called the 'Standard Theory'. This introduced and expounded the notion of DEEP STRUCTURE, which is still an essential part of the theory. Several important changes were made in the 1970s (see especially 5.5), to produce the 'Extended Standard Theory' (EST). Chomsky's position at the beginning of the 1980s is to be found in *Lectures on Government and Binding*.

It would be inappropriate in an elementary book such as this to introduce a great deal of technical detail; an attempt will be made, therefore, to explain in simple terms the main ideas associated with the theory. But it will not be possible to do justice to the present position which, inevitably, is far more complex than that of *Syntactic Structures*. It is not intended to give an historical account of the theory, but some of the ideas clearly follow from others, and the basic ideas may, therefore, be introduced in, very roughly, the order in which they were first promoted.

5.1 Transformations

Constituent structure analysis, in terms of PS grammar, taken together with all the relevant information from the lexicon allows us to generate a vast number of sentences; if we allow recursion, an infinite number can be generated. Yet it will fail to deal with some characteristics of language, e.g. discontinuity, where we need a model that either somehow allows for crossing branches, or else permits elements to be moved from one 'original' position to another. TG takes the second of these options: it has rules that permit the movement of elements. We have already noted some examples of discontinuity where this might seem appropriate. Even more obvious, perhaps, is:

> *There was a boy in the room with long hair.*

It does not require much ingenuity to suggest that *with long hair* 'belongs' with *a boy*, and has been moved from its 'original' or 'underlying' position:

> *There was a boy with long hair in the room.*

Similarly, there is ambiguity in:

> *She only passed in French.*

In one sense *only* qualifies *passed*; in another it qualifies *in*

French, and this second interpretation can be explained by the assumption that there is an 'underlying' sentence:

> *She passed only in French.*

Phrase structure grammars also fail, as we have seen, to show how sentences that look similar may in fact be very different in some way (see 4.4) or to show how sentences that look very different are, nevertheless, closely related. It is problems of this kind that may be handled in terms of transformational relations.

In the earlier literature, at least, the most important of these relations was that between active and passive sentences, for this is clearly something that the phrase structure grammars cannot account for. Let us consider two contrasting pairs of sentences. First:

> *The boy kicks the ball.*
> *The boy kicked the ball.*

The relation between these is easily handled by a phrase structure grammar. They differ only in that one has a present tense ending to the verb (*-s*), while the other has a past tense ending (*-ed*). Apart from that, they are identical in their structure and their analyses would show simply that there was a difference in the endings (the morphemes) that occur with the lexical element KICK, a difference associated with present and past tense. But the situation is very different with:

> *The boy kicked the ball.*
> *The ball was kicked by the boy.*

It is quite reasonable to argue that these two sentences are also closely related grammatically, but that the difference is not one of tense, but of voice (active and passive); this is precisely what the traditional grammars would tell us. But there is no obvious method of showing this in a phrase structure analysis. Indeed, most linguists of the structuralist school were content not to relate such pairs of active and passive sentences at all, and even to suggest that any relationship between them was purely semantic and not grammatical, i.e. that they had roughly the same meaning.

What we need is a theory that will not merely allow us to relate sentences by indicating that they are the same except for one or two elements that they contain, but will also account for the fact that the same elements occur in different places in the sentence structure. We want to be able to say that in the first sentence *the boy* occurs before the verb and *the ball* after it, while in the second *the ball* occurs before the verb and *the boy* together with *by* after it, and that the form of the verb itself is different, active in one sentence and passive in the other. (In traditional terms, *the boy* is the subject in the first sentence and *the ball* the object, while in the second sentence *the ball* is the subject, while *the boy* is neither subject nor object. (Chomsky does not make use of the terms 'subject' and object' in his technical descriptions, but although there are problems about the terms in some languages (see pp. 76–7) they are relatively uncontroversial for English, and will regularly be used in this exposition.)

If, as in the examples of discontinuity, we are to handle this relationship in terms of movement, we must decide which type of sentence, active or passive, is the more basic. The active is the obvious choice, partly because of its greater frequency in most types of English, partly because of the greater simplicity of the form of the verb, and partly for syntactic reasons. One such reason is the existence of the so-called 'agentless' passives, e.g.:

> *The man was killed.*   (cf. *The man was killed by lightning.*)

If we were to derive active sentences from passive sentences we should expect an active sentence with no 'agent':

> **Killed the man*   (cf. *Lightning killed the man.*)

By contrast, if we derive passive sentences from active sentences, we need only to allow for agents to be omitted or deleted, in order to account for the fact that passive sentences may occur with no agents, but active sentences may not.

We can derive passive sentences from active ones, then, (i) by changing the form of the verb from active to passive, (ii) by adding *by*, (iii) by moving the two NPs – the object to subject position and the subject to a position after *by*, and (iv) by deleting the NP where necessary. Since movement and change are involved, the term 'transformation' is a good one, and in the earliest form of TG the operation was described as the 'passive transformation'. (But this is an over-simplification – see p. 157.) In general, for every active sentence there is a corresponding passive sentence. (There are a few exceptions, apart from those involving agentless passives – see p. 158.) We can predict, for instance, that if the first pair of sentences below are sentences of English, so too are the second pair:

> *The committee rejected the main proposals.*
> *The teacher punished the naughty children.*
>
> *The main proposals were rejected by the committee.*
> *The naughty children were punished by the teacher.*

This point was made by Chomsky in *Syntactic Structures* in the statement (slightly modified):

> If S_1 is a grammatical sentence of the form
> $$NP_1 \ V_{act} \ NP_2$$
> then the corresponding string of the form
> $$NP_2 \ V_{pass} \ NP_1$$
> is also a grammatical sentence.

However, when we compare active and passive sentences in this way, we must take into account the selectional restrictions that hold between the NPs (or, perhaps, the nouns) and the lexical verbs. For since the first pair below does not occur, we can predict that the second does not either:

> **The thought kicked the ball.*
> **The ball kicked the boy.*
>
> **The ball was kicked by the thought.*
> **The boy was kicked by the ball.*

Moreover, it is often the case that sentences may be ruled out if the verb is changed from active to passive but the NPs are not moved, as some examples given by Chomsky show:

> *John plays golf.*
> **John is played by golf.*
>
> *John admires sincerity.*
> **John is admired by sincerity.*

The essential point that is shown here is that, with passivization, the selectional restrictions apply to the two nouns vis-à-vis the verb, but in the reverse order.

There has been some debate about the relevance of selectional restrictions as grammatical criteria (see 4.3), but it is difficult to see how any serious grammatical discussion could take place without taking them into account, or at least using them in exemplification. Yet this is not to say that selectional restrictions are part of the grammar. Sentences with impossible selectional restrictions are semantically, rather than grammatically, anomalous. Consider again Chomsky's:

Colourless green ideas sleep furiously.

This is linguistically deviant and should be ruled out by the semantics and the lexicon. But, as Chomsky himself once said, it is not ungrammatical.

There are other types of transformational relation. A very similar analysis is required to account for questions (see p. 146), if we are to relate *Is John coming?* to *John is coming* or *Has John seen Mary?* to *John has seen Mary*. Here it would be reasonable to derive the interrogative sentences from the declarative ones. The auxiliary verbs (*is* and *has* in our examples) are moved to a position before the first NP. There is a complication in that if there is no auxiliary verb in the declarative sentence, an appropriate form of the verb DO has to be introduced and placed before this NP – *John comes*, *Does John come?*, *John came*, *Did John come?* (but see below p. 158).

It is not only simple sentences that are handled in terms of transformations. Subordinate sentences will also involve such analysis. For consider the sentence:

The man I saw yesterday came to dinner.
(or *The man that I saw yesterday came to dinner.*
The man whom I saw yesterday came to dinner.)

Here we can propose that there are two basic sentences:

The man came to dinner.
I saw the man yesterday.

When the second of these is embedded in the first by a recursive rule (4.4), we need transformational rules to delete *the man* and somehow to replace the NP with *that* or *whom* in the second and third examples.

We can also deal in a similar way with:

Bill wants to meet Mary.

We can compare this to:

Bill wants John to meet Mary.

This suggests the first sentence is derived by a transformation from something like:

Bill wants [s Bill meet Mary]

Here *Bill meet Mary* is, in TG terminology, the complement of the verb *wants*, and the transformation must not only delete the second occurrence of *Bill*, but also add *to*.

The argument so far depends on the assumption that there are some sentences that are more basic than others in the sense that the others are derived from them by transformations (though this is not strictly true, as we shall see in the next section). These Chomsky referred to as 'kernel' sentences; they are, by definition, active, declarative and simple (not involving subordination or coordination).

5.2 Deep structure

In the previous section it was assumed that transformations will simply convert one sentence into another, active into passive, declarative into interrogative, or, in the case of our embedding examples, two sentences into one. This is, however, misleading for two related reasons.

First, even declarative active sentences, the kernel sentences, may have to undergo transformations, because they cannot be entirely generated by PS-rules. Consider for instance:

The man has been reading a book.

Has been reading here is present tense, perfect phase and progressive aspect (see p. 86). These three grammatical characteristics are marked, respectively, by (1) the *-s* of *has*, a form of HAVE, (ii) the verb HAVE together with the past participle of the following verb BE (*been*), and (iii) the verb BE together with the present participle, or *-ing* form, of the following verb READ. A phrase structure grammar could introduce the past tense, the perfect and the progressive as grammatical elements of the verb phrase. The way in which this was originally done was by treating them all as auxiliaries. A phrase structure rule could expand the auxiliary element into three:

Aux→Tense, Aspect, Phase

Chomsky's original version of this rule treats tense as obligatory (every verb phrase must be present or past) and the rest as optional (there may be a marker of the progressive aspect or perfect phase). Moreover, it directly introduces the formal markers of the progressive and the perfect, and does not refer to their grammatical labels. The rule is:

Aux→Tense (have + en) (be + ing)

The brackets show which elements are treated as optional. The reason for the choice of *be* and *ing* for the progressive is obvious enough, since BE and the *-ing* of the following verb are the relevant elements. For the perfect we clearly need the verb HAVE; *en* is chosen to represent the past participle ending, because it is the actual ending in, e.g. *taken*, *broken* and *been*; although it is not used with many other verbs (most of which have *-ed*), when it is used it is distinctive and contrasts with the *-ed* of past tense. The marker for tense is either *s* for present or *-ed* for past. The PS rules, then, will generate:

The man s have + en be + ing read the book

We now need a rule, a transformational rule, known as 'affix hopping' to place the ending *s*, *en* and *ing* in the position to which they belong – after the following verb – to give:

The man have + s be + en read + ing the book

There is a need for a further rule, a morphophonemic rule, to convert *have + s* into *has*. If our sentence had been *The man has read the book* we should have ended up with *read + en*, which also would have needed a similar rule to convert it to *read*, while if it had been *The man read the book*, the PS rules and the transformation would have generated *read + ed*, which also would have required conversion to *read*. These rules may seem complicated but the facts themselves are far from simple, and the rules make these facts quite explicit. Even so, the rules have been simplified for ease of exposition; in fact Chomsky's PS rule also introduced (optional) modal verbs and read:

Aux→Tense (Modal) (have + en) (be + ing)

This (along with affix hopping and the morphophonemics) would allow us to generate:

The man may have been reading the book.

Secondly, if we are to generate passive sentences, it is sensible to carry out the transformations that involve the movement of the NPs and the change in the form of the verb, before the rules of affix hopping and the morphophonemic rules. Let us simplify our sentences still further and consider only:

The man has read the book.
The book has been read by the man.

Apart from moving the NPs, all we need to do is to add the passive in the form *be + en*: we can derive the passive sentence in the following way:

(1) The man s have + en read the book
(2) The book s have + en be + en read by the man
(3) The book have + s be + en read + en by the man
(4) The book has been read by the man

(1) is the PS structure of the kernel (active) sentence. In (2) the NPs have been moved, *by* introduced and *be + en* added. (3) and (4) show the effects of affix hopping and the morphophonemic rules respectively.

It is clear from this, however, that the rules relating to passivization apply not to the (kernel) active sentences themselves, but to PS structures (kernel structures) that underlie them (before affix hopping and the morphophonemic rules). In the Standard Theory (*Aspects of the Theory of Syntax*) it was argued that there is an even 'deeper' structure than this – DEEP STRUCTURE, which is abstract, as compared with SURFACE STRUCTURE, which represents the actual forms of the language. In such a deep structure, moreover, we shall have the specification of all the relevant grammatical categories, not only of tense, modals, aspect and phase, but also of voice. The rules that generate the deep structures will also introduce the passive in the same way as the earlier rules had introduced the perfect and the progressive. The passive will be introduced, as an optional element, with '*by* Pass', and the deep structure of the passive sentence above will be something like:

The man s have + en read the book by Pass

Now if we reconsider the transformational rules of affix hopping it will be seen that those rules were obligatory. The affixes were in the wrong places and the rules had to apply if a possible sentence was to be generated. The same is true for the deep structure of the passive. The presence of Pass makes the transformations obligatory. It is said to 'trigger' rules that introduce the passive marker of the verb $be + en$, place NP_1 at the end in place of Pass itself, and place NP_2 in initial position. If the optional voice element *by* Pass is chosen, structure (2) above will be generated; if it is not, structure (1), that of the active sentence, will result.

Interrogative sentences can be generated in a similar way by introducing the (optional) element Q into the deep structure. This, too, will trigger the appropriate transformations, which include transposing NP and the first auxiliary verb (NP-AUX INVERSION) and, where necessary, the insertion of a form of the verb DO. Thus *Can John come?* is derived from *Q John can come* with transposition of *John* and *can* (plus the deletion of Q). But *Does John come?* requires also the insertion of *do* into the deep structure *Q John s come* and after that the transposition of the two elements. If our deep structures are abstract, there is an alternative way of generating interrogative sentences. We could introduce *do* as an element in the deep structure and delete it only when we do not have an interrogative. This may seem a little implausible, since it entails that *John comes* has the deep structure *John s do come*, suggesting a kernel sentence *John does come*. But in this model we do not transform from kernel structures, but from abstract deep structures, and it may be more plausible to delete an element like *do* than to introduce it by a transformation.

We can take the analysis further, by introducing other abstract elements. Let us reconsider agentless passives such as:

The man was killed.

This has no active counterpart **Killed the man*, because, except in the case of imperatives, all (simple) English sentences must have subjects. But although sentences of this type may seem evidence for transformation from active to passive with deletion of NP_1, the subject (see p. 152), there is a problem in the original version of transformation: what was the NP that was deleted? A possibility is that it was *Someone*, the corresponding active sentence being:

Someone killed the man.

But this is wrong because there is an obvious passive to this, which is not agentless:

The man was killed by someone.

There is no real problem, however, with an analysis in terms of an abstract deep structure. All that is needed is an abstract, 'dummy' or 'zero' subject, which may be symbolized as Δ, so that the deep structure of our agentless passive would be:

Δ past kill the man by Pass

The transformation triggered by Pass generates:

The man past be + en kill by Δ

A further rule deletes *by* Δ and the correct surface structure is obtained. But we have to add to our grammar the rule that carries out this deletion.

There are three points to notice about this grammatical model. First, we need rules to generate the deep structure. Now since these are, except for the presence of such elements as Pass and Q, very like our previous phrase structures, it is fairly obvious that they should be generated by PS-rules. The PS-rules, then, will not generate surface structures as they did in all earlier grammatical models, but will generate these more abstract deep structures. The surface structures will be generated only after the application of all the transformations; they are the output of the transformational rules (while the deep structures are the input). Secondly, the most important transformational rules are automatic or 'obligatory'. They are carried out only if the deep structures contain the appropriate elements, and then they must be carried out. We cannot now think in terms of having the choice whether or not to transform an active sentence into a passive one (though this was never strictly what was suggested), but only of deriving both active and passive sentences from very similar deep structures, the different order of elements in the passive being triggered by the presence of the element Pass. Thirdly, the deep structures can contain quite abstract elements, such as Pass, Q and Δ which are (and must be) deleted by the transformational rules.

This leads to a further point to be made about the dummy elements. They obviously do not occur in surface structure and it is essential, therefore, that the transformational rules delete them. But let us consider agentless passives again. We have seen that active and passive sentences differ only in the presence of *by* Pass in the deep structures. This will be introduced by an optional phrase structure rule, just like the optional rule that allows us to choose (or not to choose) to have *be* + *ing* or a modal verb. But since we are permitted to choose Δ as a deep structure subject we can generate a deep structure with Δ but without *by* Pass to give:

Δ past kill the man

If now, however, we delete the Δ to obtain the surface structure we shall arrive at the ungrammatical sentence:

Killed the man

The rules, that is to say, as they have been presented, will allow us to generate agentless active sentences as well as agentless passive ones, but these are ungrammatical because they have no (surface structure) subjects. How can this be avoided? It would be possible to say that Δ can never be generated unless *by* Pass is generated also, but to do that would greatly complicate the PS-rules, and would, in fact, make them more like transformational rules. For the phrase structure rules do no more than expand symbols without stating any conditions: they are 'context free' and do not include rules that say 'insert this only if you insert something else somewhere else'. What, then, is the alternative? The suggestion is that we have rules that 'filter out', i.e. mark as ungrammatical, any surface structures that contain dummy elements. The transformational rules will, that is to say, be allowed to generate Δ *killed the man*, but the filters will not allow it to be included in the grammatical sentences generated by the grammar. This has some plausibility – it says, in effect, that some sentences do not have deep structure subjects, but that all sentences have surface structure subjects, and that, if the deep surface subject is unstated or unknown, the surface sentence must be passive, and that the corresponding active one is ungrammatical. We shall return later to this notion of (surface structure) filters – the devices that rule out certain surface structures as ungrammatical.

In addition to the interrogatives that we have just been considering, English (as well as other languages) has what are called '*wh*-questions' (as contrasted with '*yes/no* questions'). These all involve the *wh*-WORDS *who*, *what*, *which*, *why*, etc., and even *how* (though it alone does not begin with *wh*-). With these it can be argued that we need transformations not only to transpose the subject of the auxiliary verb, but in many cases to move the NP containing the *wh*-word to initial position ('*wh*-MOVEMENT'). Thus for:

> *What did you buy?*
> *Which book did you buy?*

we would propose the deep structures:

> You past buy what
> You past buy which book

However, the argument for these deep structures does not rest on a comparison with kernel sentences as it does for *yes/no*-questions. The point, rather, is that they show that *what* and *which books* are the objects of *buy*, not the subjects, in spite of the fact that they occur before the verb. Deep structure, that is to say, will indicate subjects and objects when surface structures disguise them. This is, perhaps, the most important justification of deep structures and one to which we shall return (pp. 166–71).

It would be sufficient simply to compare the sentences above with:

> *You bought it.*
> *You bought these books.*

More sophisticatedly we could argue as follows. BUY is a transitive verb and requires an object. If *what* and *which books* are not the objects, we imply the ungrammatical **You bought* and we have no grammatical status to give to either of the NPs. Equally we cannot explain, if these are not the objects, why we cannot say **What did you buy the groceries?* or **Which book did you buy the groceries?* Of course, common sense tells us that *what* and *which book* are the objects of *buy*, and that the proposed deep structure is, therefore, justified, but it is always useful to be able to provide arguments of this kind to justify the analysis at a formal level. Movement of the NPs is, of course, required only when they are objects of the verb. If the *wh*-NP is the subject no movement is required, e.g.:

> *Which book is on the table?*

Deep structures can equally be used to deal with recursion involving embedded sentences. We have already seen that with both complements and relative clauses we need some transformational rules (see pp. 154–5). We also need to know precisely where the embedded sentences are to be positioned and this is something that can be done quite easily by the (deep structure) PS rules. In *Bill wants to meet Mary* we simply treat *Bill meet Mary* as the complement of *wants*, as an S generated by the PS rule VP→V – S (p. 143). The phrase structure tree will, then, be:

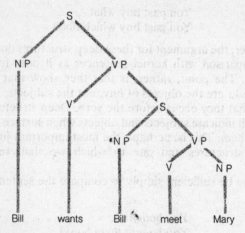

Or, in simplified form, we can show this as:

Bill wants [s Bill meet Mary]

Transformational rules obligatorily delete the second *Bill*, which is identical with the subject of *wants* in the main clause (see p. 155), and add *to*. (For simplicity we shall, in future, ignore the issue of *to* and insert it in the simplified deep structures.)

Slightly different, but involving similar principles, is the analysis of:

I persuaded the doctor to examine John.

The deep structure of this is:

I persuaded the doctor [s the doctor to examine John]

Again the second occurrence of the identical NPs (*the doctor*) is deleted; here, however, it is identical with the object, not the subject, of the verb of the main clause (*persuaded*).

The rule that deletes the second NP in these examples is

known as EQUI-NP DELETION. It depends, however, not simply
on the identity of the form of the NPs, but on a feature that is
not strictly a matter of grammar at all, the fact that they are CO-
REFERENTIAL, i.e. that they refer to the same person or thing. If
the persons referred to by the second occurrence of *John* or *the
doctor* were not the same as those referred to by the first, we
should not delete. For it is perfectly possible that Bill Smith
wants Bill Brown to meet Mary, and there is nothing odd about
the sentence (where no deletion has taken place):

> *Bill wants Bill to meet Mary.*

(Similarly, I could persuade Doctor Brown that Doctor Smith
should examine John. English does not, however, similarly
permit:

> **I persuaded the doctor the doctor to examine John.*

We can, of course, say instead:

> *I persuaded the doctor that the doctor should examine John.*

But we should probably need a different deep structure for this
second sentence, and have the first 'filtered out', see p. 178). To
ensure that Equi-NP Deletion applies where the NPs are co-
referential, these NPs are co-indexed, i.e. marked with identical
subscript numerals, e.g.:

> Bill$_1$ wants [$_s$ Bill$_1$ to meet Mary]
> I persuaded the doctor$_1$ [$_s$ the doctor$_1$ to examine John]

Part of the justification of this analysis is that it helps to
explain:

> *Bill wants to help himself.*
> *I persuaded the doctor to help himself.*

These may be contrasted with:

> *Bill wants to help him.*
> *I persuaded the doctor to help him.*

Pronouns such as *himself* and *him* usually have antecedents,
NPs to which they refer, or, more strictly, with which they are
co-referential, and there is a difference between a reflexive
pronoun such as *himself* and an ordinary pronoun such as *him*,
in that the reflexives usually refer to an NP in the same clause as

themselves, whereas the other pronouns do not (see p. 59). This is clear enough in the contrast of:

> *Bill helped him./Bill helped himself.*

If, however, we analyse the sentences in terms of their surface structures, we find that the reflexive pronouns are not in the same clause as their antecedents:

> Bill wants [to help himself]
> I persuaded the doctor [to help himself]

But there is no problem if we argue that the NPs in the subordinate clause have been deleted and that the deep structures (showing the full co-reference) are:

> Bill$_1$ wants [$_S$ Bill$_1$ help himself$_1$]
> I persuaded the doctor$_1$ [$_S$ the doctor$_1$ help himself$_1$]

Let us now consider two kinds of embedded sentences that use *wh*-words. First, we have INDIRECT QUESTIONS of the kind:

> *He asked me what I bought.*
> *He asked me which book I bought.*

Like the (direct) questions we discussed earlier (p. 16), these involve *wh*-movement of object NPs. The deep structures would be:

> He asked me [$_S$ I bought what]
> He asked me [$_S$ I bought which books]

There is one difference: with indirect questions there is usually no transposition of the subject and an auxiliary. English does not normally allow:

> *?He asked me what had I bought.*
> *?He asked me which book had I bought.*

It is not only *wh*-questions that have these indirect question counterparts. The same is true of *yes/no* questions, though the indirect counterparts have either *whether* (which is clearly a *wh*-word) or *if*:

> *He asked me whether/if John could come.*

It could be argued (and has been argued though not in the Standard Theory) that in deep structure all questions, direct or indirect, have *wh*-words. For *yes/no* questions the *wh*-word is *whether*, as evidenced in the indirect questions. In direct questions, though it is present in deep structure, it is deleted in surface structure. The deep structure of *Can John come?* would be, then:

Whether John can come

This would restore the symmetry and do away with the need of the rather artificial dummy Q.

Relative clauses also involve *wh*-words. It is simplest to assume that all relative clauses contain *wh*-words, though these may be deleted in surface structure in e.g. *The man I saw*, or replaced by *that* as in *The man that I saw*. If so, the deep structure of the sentence we considered earlier (*The man (whom/that) I saw yesterday came to dinner*) might be:

The man₁ [s I saw wh- the man₁ yesterday] came to dinner

More simply, perhaps, it might be:

The man₁ [s I saw whom₁ yesterday] came to dinner

In either case, the *wh*-NP is moved to initial position in the clause and may be deleted. It is to be noticed, however, that where the relative pronoun is omitted it can only be interpreted as the object of the verb. It is not usual to say:

*The man arrived yesterday came to dinner.

In other words, deletion can take place only where there is *wh*-movement.

The Standard Theory (see p. 150) appealed to many scholars for a long time, not only because it provided a fairly simple and coherent account of syntax, but also because of the claim that deep structures, in addition to their syntactic role of providing the 'input' to the transformations, also determined the semantic interpretation of sentences. For these deep structures contained all the necessary grammatical and lexical information, not merely the phrase structures with specification of the grammatical categories, together with abstract categories such as passive and Q and symbols to indicate what sentences are embedded, but also all the lexical items together with the selectional restrictions in which they are involved. It was highly plausible to suggest that such structures contained everything that was needed to lead us to the meaning of these sentences.

One important point was that the transformations themselves

could not change meaning. Any difference in the meaning between a question and a statement was predictable from the presence or absence of Q. By contrast, a theory that simply envisaged the transformation of a (kernel) declarative sentence into an interrogative one would imply that the transformation itself brought about the change of meaning. With deep structures and elements such as Q, all meaning could be located in one component of the grammar.

In particular the notion of deep structure allows us to 'keep track' of the co-referentiality of NPs, even when they have been omitted or deleted. This often allows us to explain why sentences that look alike are nevertheless very different in some way. Their similarities are in their surface structures; their deep structures are different. Consider, for instance:

> *I wanted the doctor to examine John.*
> *I persuaded the doctor to examine John.*

Intuitively, we would wish to say that what I wanted was for the doctor to examine John, whereas the object of my persuasion was not for the doctor to examine John, but the doctor. We might, then, suggest that the deep structures were different:

> I wanted [$_S$ the doctor to examine John]
> I persuaded the doctor$_1$ [$_S$ the doctor$_1$ to examine John]

Equi-NP Deletion will then ensure that with the deletion of the second *the doctor* the surface structures will be alike.

This proposal has so far been based solely upon notional or semantic criteria. It is essential that it should be justified grammatically, if it is to be accepted. There are several points that may be adduced. First, we can replace the embedded sentence with a passive:

> *I wanted John to be examined by the doctor.*
> *I persuaded John to be examined by the doctor.*

However, whereas in the first sentence there is little change of meaning and we can reasonably argue that the only difference is that the embedded sentence has been passivized, in the second something more drastic has occurred. Indeed, if we had chosen different lexical items, the sentence with the passive would have to be ruled out with PERSUADE (but not with WANT):

I persuaded/wanted the doctor to buy the book.
**I persuaded the book to be bought by the doctor.*
I wanted the book to be bought by the doctor.

If we refer to deep structures the explanation is clear. With PERSUADE the object of the verb and the subject of the embedded sentence must be the same, and Equi-NP deletion must take place. If we passivize the embedded sentence, we find that the subject is no longer *the doctor*, but *John* or *the book*, and Equi-NP deletion cannot take place. For Equi-NP deletion to take place with the embedded passive sentence where *John* is the subject, we need the quite different deep structure:

I persuaded John$_1$ [$_S$ John$_1$ to be examined by the doctor]

None of these arguments apply to WANT, which is, therefore, unaffected by the passivization of the embedded sentence.

Secondly, we can passivize the main clause with PERSUADE, but not with WANT:

The doctor was persuaded to examine John.
**The doctor was wanted to examine John.*

This is easy to explain in terms of deep structure. In our active sentence with PERSUADE, *the doctor* was the object and so can become the subject of the passive; but this was not so with WANT.

The verb PROMISE involves yet another type of co-referentiality relation. For with

John promised Mary to come.

the normal interpretation is that John made a promise to Mary, (so that *Mary* is the object of *promised*), but that what he promised was that he, not Mary, should come (so that *John* is the subject of the embedded clause). The deep structure is, then:

John$_1$ promised Mary [$_S$ John$_1$ come]

If this is so we have Equi-NP deletion involving the subject of the main clause (not the object as with PERSUADE) and the subject of the embedded clause.

Another pair of examples that was widely quoted to show how deep structures can be used to indicate subjects and objects is:

> *John is easy to please.*
> *John is eager to please.*

The surface structures appear to be the same but there are, two differences. First, with *easy* it is John who is pleased, while with *eager* it is John who pleases, i.e. John is the object of *please* in one (the subject being unstated), the subject in the other. Secondly, whereas John can be said to be eager, he cannot be said to be easy (except in a different, colloquial, sense). These points are brought out clearly with different NPs:

> *The book is easy to read.*
> **The book is eager to read.*
> **The boy is easy to read.*
> *The boy is eager to read.*

Moreover, we can say

> *It is easy to please John.*

but not (except in a different sense)

> *It is eager to please John.*

Our deep structures need to show two things, the different functions of *John* in the embedded sentence and the fact that the embedded sentence is itself the subject (the *it*) of *is easy*. This is simple enough with something like:

> $[_S \Delta$ to please John] is easy
> John$_1$ is eager $[_S$John$_1$ to please]

For the second sentence Equi-NP deletion (of *John*) will give the correct surface structure. For the first, however, we need to do three things: we must move *to please* to the end of the sentence (this movement is not unlike the movement we suggested for some of the discontinuity examples on p. 150); we must delete the dummy Δ; and we must indicate in the surface structure analysis that *John* is the subject of the verb of the main sentence (here *is*). This movement of a noun phrase from a position in an embedded clause to a position in the main clause is known as RAISING. One important result of this is that *John* agrees with *is*. Had the NP been *the boys* the verb would have been *are* (*The boys are easy to please*). The first deep structure will also generate:

Pleasing John is easy.
It is easy to please John.

The first of these merely requires a rule to generate *pleasing* instead of *to please*; the second needs a rule to account for *it* and a rule to move *to please John* to the end of the sentence. The movement is simple enough; the account of *it* requires either that we write *it* in the deep structure and delete *it* in all the other sentences, or that we have a rule that inserts *it* here after *to please John* has been moved out of subject position.

There are inevitably problems, because language is seldom tidy. We need to say more to explain:

Columbus is believed by everyone to have discovered America.

The fact that the main clause has been passivized suggests that BELIEVE here is like PERSUADE, but this is unsatisfactory for two reasons. First, if we follow the argument for PERSUADE, we shall establish the deep structure:

Everyone believes Columbus₁ [s Columbus₁ to have discovered America] by Pass

But the semantic interpretation will then suggest that, just as it was the doctor who was persuaded, so too it is Columbus that is believed (not the fact that he discovered America). Secondly, if we consider the corresponding sentence with an active main clause, we find that as with WANT, but not PERSUADE, we can passivize the embedded sentence with little change of meaning:

Everyone believes Columbus to have discovered America.
Everyone believes America to have been discovered by
*   Columbus.*

This strongly points to the conclusion that the deep structures required here are:

Everyone believes [s Columbus to have discovered America (by
Pass)]

Columbus does not appear here as the object of *believes*.

This, however, fails to explain how *Columbus* can be the subject of the (passive) main clause in the first example we considered. For this we again need to postulate a rule of Raising whereby the subject of the embedded clause is raised to the main clause. One way of achieving this is to say that the subject of the embedded clause is raised to become the object of the main clause and that then the main clause is passivized:

> Everyone believes [s Columbus to have discovered America] by Pass
> →Everyone believes Columbus [s to have discovered America] by Pass (Raising)
> →Columbus is believed by everyone to have discovered America (Passivization)

This was the generally accepted solution and was known as 'subject to object raising'.

An alternative solution is to treat the whole of the embedded clause *Columbus to have discovered America* as an NP and as the object of BELIEVE. If that is so, passivization of the main clause will move this embedded clause to the position of subject to give:

> Everyone believes [s Columbus to have discovered America] by Pass
> →[s Columbus to have discovered America] is believed by everyone

Columbus can now be raised to become the subject of the main clause in surface structure ('subject to subject raising'), while *to have discovered America* is moved to the end of the sentence.

This second solution has the advantage that it is very similar, in its final stages, to the analysis of *John is easy to please*, where the embedded sentence is the subject of the main sentence. There is, however, a difference in that *John* is the object of the verb, whereas *Columbus* is the subject. But there is an even closer similarity with the analysis proposed for verbs like SEEM, as in:

> *John seems to have seen Mary.*

Here we find that there is a passive with very little difference in meaning:

> *Mary seems to have been seen by John.*

Clearly these are very unlike *John wants to see Mary* and *John wants to be seen by Mary*. How then are they to be explained? The simplest solution is to say that the embedded sentence is, in deep structure, the subject of the main verb:

[s John to have seen Mary (by Pass)] seems

If *by* Pass is not chosen, *John* is raised to become the subject of *seems*. If *by* Pass is chosen, passivization will yield:

[s Mary to have seen by John] seems

Mary may now be raised to become the subject of *seems*. Once again we have 'subject to subject raising', as in our second solution for the *Columbus* example. With that example too, we may passivize the embedded sentence, for we can also say:

> *America is believed by everyone to have been discovered by Columbus.*

This is easily generated from:

[s Columbus to have discovered America by Pass] is believed by everyone

Passivization yields:

[s America to have been discovered by Columbus] is believed by everyone

Once again the subject (*America*) is raised and the remainder of the embedded clause (*to have been discovered by Columbus*) is moved to the end of the sentence.

In the early days of tg too much was claimed for transformations and deep structures. It was argued, for instance, that they are needed to account for the ambiguity of:

> *Flying planes can be dangerous.*
> *Visiting relatives can be a nuisance.*

While it is perfectly true that two different deep structures can be assigned to each of these, involving Δ *fly planes* or *Planes fly* and Δ *visit relatives* or *Relatives visit* (once again a matter of subjects and objects), the ambiguity need not be left unstated in a purely phrase structure analysis. It is easy enough to prove that in one sense *flying* and *visiting* are the head nouns, but that in the other *planes* and *relatives* are. Simple agreement with the verb shows this:

> *Flying planes is/are dangerous.*
> *Visiting relatives is/are a nuisance.*

More important, perhaps, was the quite basic argument in *Syntactic Structures* that all coordination (with conjunctions such as *and*) can be dealt with by transformational rules. Chomsky had argued that

The liner sailed down and the tugboat chugged up the river.

was derived from conjoining:

The liner sailed down the river.
The tugboat chugged up the river.

This can be dealt with in a deep structure analysis by permitting S to be expanded to S *and* S and then by rules that delete one occurrence of identical elements. But there are difficulties of all kinds here. It may, for instance, seem reasonable to relate

John and Bill went to London.
to   *John went to London. Bill went to London.*

But we cannot provide a similar analysis for:

John and Bill met in the street.
(*John met in the street.   *Bill met in the street.)

It is now generally agreed that coordination is a matter of phrase structure – that an NP can be NP *and* NP.

Another suggestion was that all attributive adjectives could be derived by transformations from sentences with predicative ones (see p. 61). Thus, *The little boy* would be generated from *The boy$_1$ [The boy$_1$ is little]*. Unfortunately, there is considerable mismatch between the predicative and attributive uses of adjectives, as we have already noted (pp. 60–62). We should have to block the generation of *The well boy from *The boy is well* and, conversely, find a different way of generating *A heavy smoker*, since this is not derivable from *The smoker is heavy*, while *The right girl* and *The girl is right*, though both possible, are clearly not to be related transformationally.

5.3 Constraints and filters

It was suggested in the previous section that *wh*-questions may involve not only NP-Aux inversion, but also *wh*-fronting, the movement of the *wh*-NP from a late position in the clause to the front of it. Thus the sentence:

Which books has Jill bought?

is derived by such movement from the deep structure:

Jill has bought [NP which books]

The examples we considered involved only one clause, and the *wh*-NP was, therefore, moved only to initial position in that clause. But a *wh*-NP can also be moved from an embedded clause to the front of the whole sentence, before the main clause and wholly outside the embedded clause of which it is part in deep structure. Thus we may say:

Which books did Bill say that Jill has bought?

The deep structure is:

Bill said [S that Jill bought [NP which books]]

It can even be moved from a multiply embedded clause:

Which books do you think Bill said that Mary hopes that Jill has bought?

Yet there are structures from which it is not possible to move an NP by *wh*-fronting. For instance, we cannot say:

*Which books does he know the man who bought?

This is, on reflection, a little surprising, for we can say:

He knows the man who bought these books.

We should expect, therefore, that we have the deep structure:

He knows the man [S who bought [NP which books]]

It ought to be possible to generate the sentence by means of *wh*-movement, but it is not. We need, then, to explain why a *wh*-NP cannot be fronted in this example. The simplest answer is that we cannot move a *wh*-NP out of a relative clause (*who bought which books* in deep structure). It has been suggested that relative clauses are 'islands', from which elements may not be moved elsewhere, and that what prevents such movement is an ISLAND CONSTRAINT.

There would appear to be other islands for, in a similar way, we cannot say:

*What does he believe the claim that she painted?

Yet we can say:

>*He believes the claim that she painted this.*

There would be no problem if *the claim* were omitted, for both of the following are possible:

>*He believes that she painted this.*
>*What does he believe that she painted?*

Similarly, we may contrast:

>*What don't you accept that he did?*
>**What don't you accept the belief that he did?*

This second island constraint involves all clauses with NPs such as *the claim*, *the fact*, *the belief* followed by clauses introduced by *that*; these have been called 'noun complement clauses'.

It was once suggested that the constraints on movement from relative clauses and noun complement clauses could be governed by the principle that an NP can never be moved out from another NP. In our examples, it is clear enough that the relative clause together with its antecedent (*the man who bought . . .*) and the noun complement clauses (*the claim that she painted . . ., the belief that he did . . .*) are NPs, and the *wh*-NP would have been moved from inside this constituent. It was further claimed that constituents can never be moved out of other constituents of the same kind (not just NPs), a principle that was known as the A-OVER-A PRINCIPLE.

There are, however, several objections to this proposal. First, it is in fact possible to move some *wh*-NPs from other NPs as shown by:

>*What doesn't he approve of my doing?*

Here there is movement from *my doing what*, but this constituent is clearly an NP. Secondly, the proposal has to assume that *that Jill has bought these books* is not an NP in the sentence:

>*Bill said that Jill has bought these books.*

It would, that is to say, reject the traditional description of it as a noun clause, the object of *said*, for we can move NPs from this (*Which books did Bill say that Jill has bought?*). Yet such clauses function as subjects, where they must surely be NPs:

>*That Jill has bought these books is quite extraordinary.*

It would seem reasonable, then, to treat the clause as an NP when it occurs after *said*. If so, the A-over-A principle should apply. Thirdly, it is not only NPs but also other types of constituents that appear to be affected by the constraints on relative clauses and noun complement clauses. An adjectival phrase can be moved to sentence initial position:

> *Handsome though he is, I don't like him.*

It can be moved out of a *that* clause:

> *Handsome though I believe that he is, . . .*

Yet it cannot be moved out of a relative clause or a noun complement clause:

> *Handsome though I have met someone who is, . . .*
> *Handsome though I believe the claim that he is, . . .*

Similar considerations hold for an adverbial clause:

> *Tomorrow, he will meet the Queen.*
> *Tomorrow, I believe he will meet the Queen.*
> *Tomorrow, I know someone who will meet the Queen.*
> *Tomorrow, I believe the claim he will meet the Queen.*

For all the asterisked examples there is a possible sentence without the movement.

Although the A-over-A principle does not seem to provide an explanation, it can be pointed out that relative clauses and noun complement clauses are alike in that both consist of an NP and a following clause. They can be described as COMPLEX NPs and the two island constraints that affect them can be subsumed under a single COMPLEX NP CONSTRAINT, that says that an element may not be moved out of a complex NP.

There are other types of subordinate clauses from which elements may not be moved. For brevity of exposition only examples of *wh*-movement will be given here, but there are other kinds of elements that cannot be moved, as the reader can check. First, indirect questions (embedded questions), which are themselves introduced by *wh*-words, are also islands:

> *What did he ask whether you bought?*
> (cf. *He asked whether you bought this.*)
> *Who doesn't he know when I met?*
> (cf. *He doesn't know when I met her.*)

Then there are clauses that function as the subjects of other clauses such as:

That he reads books is obvious to everyone.

Yet *wh*-movement is not permitted here:

*What that he reads is obvious to everyone?

If the embedded clause is moved to the end of the main clause and replaced by *it* we have the sentence:

It is obvious to everyone that he reads books.

Surprisingly, with this structure, *wh*-movement is possible:

What is it obvious to everyone that he reads?

Perhaps we can do no more than list the kinds of islands, and so have a different constraint for each. It was in this spirit that the two constraints we have just been considering were known as the *wh*-ISLAND constraint and the SENTENTIAL SUBJECT CONSTRAINT.

Although the A-over-A principle seems not to work, search for more general principles goes on. More recently Chomsky has discussed the SUBJACENCY CONDITION. According to this, NP and S are BOUNDARY NODES, in the sense that they indicate constituents with specific types of 'boundaries', such that an element cannot be moved across two such boundaries by a single movement rule. It cannot, for instance, be moved out of an S and an NP at the same time. This condition would deal quite simply with the complex NP constraint, for complex NPs involve clauses within noun phrases, as can be seen quite clearly from the deep structures of the examples that were discussed:

He knows [$_{NP}$ the man [$_S$ who bought [$_{NP}$ which books]]]
He believes [$_{NP}$ the claim [$_S$ that she painted [$_{NP}$ what]]]

If *which books* and *what* are moved to initial position by *wh*-movement they will be moved out of both NP and S and the condition will be violated.

It may also account for the sentential subject constraint, if, as seems reasonable, sentential subjects are both S and NP. The deep structure of the examples we considered above in relation to this constraint would be:

[$_{NP}$ [$_S$ that he reads what]] is obvious to everyone

Movement of *what* out of the embedded clause, to become the subject of *is*, would violate the subjacency condition.

There is, however, one serious counter example. We may recall:

> *Which books do you think that Bill said that Mary hopes that Jill has bought?*

Now the deep structure would be:

> You think [$_{s_1}$ that Bill said [$_{s_2}$ that Mary hopes [$_{s_3}$ that Jill bought which books]]]

If *which books* is moved, it will be moved over three S boundaries and so breach the subjacency condition. Some scholars have been content to allow that this particular movement is 'unbounded', i.e. not affected by the subjacency condition. Chomsky, however, adduces arguments, which, in effect, allow the *wh*-NP to be moved three times, each time over one boundary only. But such arguments are highly technical and complex, if not somewhat artificial and possibly circular, and cannot be discussed here.

There are other, different, constraints. One involves coordinate structures. For we cannot say:

> *Who does he like Bill and?*

Yet we might have expected a deep structure:

> He likes Bill and $_{NP}$ who

Equally we cannot move any NP in structures corresponding to:

> *John likes Bill and hates Fred.*

Neither of the following is possible:

> *Who does John like Bill and hate?*
> *Who does John like and hate Fred?*

The constraint does not affect only *wh*-NPs. It affects adjectival and adverbial phrases too:

> *Handsome though he is brave and, I don't like him.*
> *The next day he will meet the Queen tomorrow and.*

For all of these we need a COORDINATED STRUCTURE constraint.

We have been considering constraints on rules, on transformations, or more precisely, on particular movement rules. We prevent ungrammatical sentences from being generated by preventing certain rules from applying to certain types of structure. There is another, quite different, way of preventing the grammar from generating ungrammatical sentences. It is to allow the rules to generate them and then to 'filter' them out. Instead of making reference to deep structures to see whether the rules can be allowed to apply, we look at the surface structures and rule them out if certain conditions do not apply. These conditions are themselves the 'filters'. We have already noted one type of filter – a sentence with a dummy such as Δ is filtered out (p. 160). Most of the work on filters involves fairly complex argumentation, though the idea is simple enough. Inevitably, it is fairly 'model specific', in the sense that precisely what filters are needed will depend on the choice of the actual generative model being used, for we need to filter out structures only if the rules of the model have generated them. If the rules do not generate sentences without subjects, for instance, there is no need to exclude them by the use of a filter.

Let us briefly consider a few of the filters that have been suggested. One is the EMPTY SUBJECT FILTER, an updated version of the more general filter that excludes subjectless sentences by the use of Δ. This filter will also rule out:

Who did he say that was coming?

Movement of *who* here leaves *was coming* without a subject. By contrast we can move *who* from object position without forming an ungrammatical sentence, because there is a subject:

Who did he say that he saw?

But baldly stated, this filter will not account for the incomplete sentences we discussed on p. 69 such as *Coming?* or *Found them?* And we shall need some device to account for the grammaticality of sentences where the subject of the embedded clause has been deleted by Equi-NP deletion, e.g. as in *John wants (   ) to come* (but see pp. 187–8).

Another example of the need for a filter is the fact that we cannot say:

Is that she is coming obvious?

For we can say:

That she is coming is obvious.

It is fairly clear here that *that she is coming* is the subject of *is*, and that, therefore, it is an NP (as well as an S):

[NP [S that she is coming]] is obvious

If so, NP-Aux inversion ought to apply to produce the interrogative sentence. It would be difficult to invent a constraint to prevent NP-Aux inversion from taking place, but we might, instead, suggest that a clause such as *that she is coming* is not permitted in the middle of another clause such as *. . . is obvious*. The facts are complex and not altogether clear, but it was originally suggested that we need here the INTERNAL CLAUSE FILTER.

The notion of filters has appeared in many versions of TG; in the most recent version it is stated in terms of quite complex and very technical proposals. It may well be that a generative grammar cannot, without enormous complexity and a vast number of constraints, succeed in generating only grammatical sentences, and that it is, therefore, easier to have fairly general and simple rules that will generate both grammatical and ungrammatical sentences and to rule out the latter by means of (surface structure) filters. It has long been recognized that it is easier to specify what is ungrammatical than to write an explicit grammar that would generate 'only and all the grammatical sentences' of a language. Nevertheless, this latter aim, which was originally the main aim of TG, is an entirely laudable one, and it will be unfortunate if it has to be abandoned. A positive grammar is intellectually more satisfying than a negative one.

One further point emerges from this. Constraints and filters have the same ultimate purpose, to 'block' ungrammatical sentences, though they work at different stages in the generative model, one preventing rules from applying, the other excluding sentences after the application of the rules. But ought we to have both types of mechanism in a single model?

5.4 *Problems of deep structure*

The Standard Theory is, in general, an attractive, coherent and relatively uncomplicated TG model, and, although Chomsky's present position is rather different, the notion of deep structure is still very important. Yet there are considerable difficulties with deep structure as proposed in this model. We shall consider just three of the many arguments presented against it.

First, there are other relations between sentences of a seemingly transformational kind that ought, perhaps, to be accounted for in deep structure. We may compare:

> *John opened the door with a key.*
> *The key opened the door.*
> *The door opened.*

A similar trio is:

> *The boy broke the window with a stone.*
> *The stone broke the window.*
> *The window broke.*

It could be argued that if, in the first example, we symbolize *John*, *the door* and *the key* as NP_1, NP_2 and NP_3 we have transformational rules to delete certain NPs and move others:

$$NP_1 - V - NP_2 \text{ with } NP_3$$
$$\rightarrow NP_3 - V - NP_2$$
$$\rightarrow NP_2 - V$$

This, in effect but not in the formalization, is what Charles Fillmore suggested in the model known as 'Case Grammar'. He referred to the relevant NPs as being in the AGENTIVE, OBJECTIVE and INSTRUMENTAL case and suggested an underlying deep structure in these terms, together with transformational rules to generate the correct surface structures.

The case system can be considerably extended. We need not only agentive and objective cases, but also DATIVE (*the boy*) to account for:

> *I gave the boy the book.*
> *I gave the book to the boy.*

Similarly, perhaps, we need a LOCATIVE case to relate:

> *It is windy in Chicago.*
> *Chicago is windy.*

Moreover, there is a contrast between:

> *I painted the picture frame.*
> *I painted the picture.*

In the first, *the picture frame* merely indicates what undergoes painting and is objective; in the second, *the picture* refers to something that is created by the painting and is FACTITIVE (though this sentence could conceivably have the other sense too).

A further extension involves the use of different verbs. With SEE the subject is not an agent – he does not 'act', whereas with LOOK AT he takes positive action. We may, therefore, argue that the NPs with SEE are dative and objective, but with LOOK AT agentive and objective as in:

> *The man saw the dog.*
> *The man looked at the dog.*

Fillmore's case theory requires a deep structure that incorporates more directly semantic information. But such a deep structure cannot be purely syntactic, as Chomsky maintained it should be.

To some degree Fillmore's arguments are not valid. It does not follow that, because one can offer analysis of this kind, it must be preferred to Chomsky's deep structure analysis. For it is perfectly possible to state all the semantic relations in the lexicon, not in the syntax. We merely recognize that subjects have an agentive meaning with some verbs, but not with others (see p. 75), that objects of a verb such as PAINT may refer to entities that are merely affected or actually created, and that subjects of verbs such as OPEN may be agents, instruments or merely semantic 'objects'. But there is still an important issue. With verbs like OPEN and BREAK, and others such as RING, we find that we have trios of sentences which seem to be related in a way very like that of active and passive. Why should they not be handled in terms of transformations and deep structures? A partial answer is that this kind of relationship holds only for a small number of lexical items. It does not hold, for instance, for HIT:

> *The boy hit the girl with a stick.*
> *The stick hit the girl.*
> **The girl hit.*

By contrast, there are very few restrictions on the verbs that function in the active–passive relationship. Yet one may still wonder whether this means that the relationships for these verbs are not to be treated as matters of deep structure. Is it inconceivable that there may not be a single level of deep structure, but that the level is 'deeper' for some verbs than for others?

Other scholars made their own, less plausible, excursions into more semantic and more lexically based deep structures; their theoretical viewpoint was known as 'generative semantics'. One well-known argument concerned the verb KILL, for which it was suggested that there is a deep structure involving something like:

X cause [$_S$ Y become [$_S$ Y not alive]]

Thus the PS structure for *The soldier killed the enemy* would be:

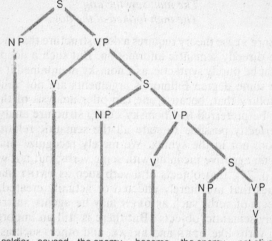

The soldier caused the enemy$_1$ become the enemy$_1$ not alive

There would then be rules to delete (Equi-NP deletion) one occurrence of *the enemy* and to 'collapse' the phrase structure, replacing *caused-become-not alive* with *killed*. The chief argument in favour of this analysis is the fact that the sentence *The soldier almost killed the enemy* may be ambiguous in three ways: he shot at him but missed; he hit him so that he nearly died (but recovered); and he hit him so that he was reduced to a (permanent) state of near death. These can be accounted for by postulating that *almost* is attached to *caused*, *become* and *not alive* respectively. However, it can also be argued that all of this should be dealt with in the semantics and not in what we might refer to as the 'pseudo-syntax' of KILL. Moreover, this may work for KILL, but it will probably not work for DESTROY. For although *almost destroyed* would seem to be ambiguous in the same three ways, it would be far less plausible to analyse DESTROY as 'cause to become destroyed'. Analyses of this kind do not seriously undermine Chomsky's deep structure, though they may suggest that the line between semantics and syntax cannot be clearly drawn.

Much more serious are arguments that show that deep structure is not always a basis for semantic interpretation. For the suggestion that deep structure may provide all that is needed for this is one of the most attractive aspects of the Standard Theory. A problem arises with the 'logical words' in English, the QUANTIFIERS (such as *many* and *few*) and the negatives. For let us compare:

> *Many men read few books.*
> *Few books are read by many men.*

According to the Standard Theory, these will have the same deep structure except that the second, the passive, will also have the element *by* Pass. Yet the two sentences have, on their most obvious interpretations, clear differences of meaning that cannot be easily accounted for by the absence or presence of the passive element. The first says, in effect, that a lot of men are illiterate and read very little, the second that very few books are bestsellers. The reason for the difference in meaning here lies in the order of the words *many* and *few*; for the order of such words usually indicates what logicians call the 'scope' of logical symbols. The first sentence says that there are many men that read few books, while the second says there are few books that are read by many men. Now the passive transformation changes the order of the two NPs and their quantifiers with them, thus ensuring that their scope, in so far as it is indicated by the order of the words, is reversed. There is a similar issue with *many* and *not* in:

> *Many arrows didn't hit the target.*
> *The target wasn't hit by many arrows.*

The first says of the arrows that many missed the target, the second of the target that it was relatively untouched by the arrows.

In fact, we do not need quantifiers and negatives to show that there may be a difference in meaning between related active and passive sentences. Chomsky himself noted the difference between:

> *Beavers build dams.*
> *Dams are built by beavers.*

The first merely says that it is a characteristic of beavers that they build dams; the second suggests, incorrectly, that it is a characteristic of dams that they are built by beavers.

The only plausible solution to these problems is to abandon the claim that deep structure determines the semantic interpretation. For it is the relative position of NPs in surface structure that determines the meanings that we have discussed. Moreover, there are other surface structure features, notably those of stress and intonation, that considerably affect meaning, and it would be very difficult indeed, if not impossible, to set up deep structures that would account for both the meaning and the surface structures relevant to such features.

Chomsky has now concluded that the two characteristics of deep structures – that they initiate the transformations and that they provide all the information for meaning – are (or can be, in theory) quite independent. At first he suggested that some semantic interpretation might be determined by surface structure, e.g. that which is related to the logical words, intonation and stress, while the rest was still determined by deep structure. More recently, he has argued that all semantic interpretation can be determined by surface structure, provided it is modified in certain fundamental ways.

5.5. Traces and binding

We now turn to consider briefly, and in a very simplified form, some of the basic ideas of Chomsky's present position, in which he relates semantic interpretation to surface structures.

It is obvious that surface structures as they have been presented in the previous sections cannot form the basis of semantic interpretation. They could not, for instance, account for the difference between *John is easy to please* and *John is eager to please*, or between the semantic–syntactic characteristics of PERSUADE and WANT (pp. 166–9). They would not even explain, in very obvious terms, why we cannot say *What did you buy the book*, unless they can show that *what* is the object of *buy* and has somehow been moved from object position. Yet the explanations were all simply and clearly given in the deep structure analysis that is now to be rejected as a basis for the semantics.

Part of Chomsky's solution is to 'enrich' the surface structures with information that relates to the deep structures, by introducing 'empty' elements that have no realization in the actual

Transformational Generative Grammar   185

surface structures. But such enriched surface structures are, obviously, not really surface structures at all, and Chomsky refers to them as 'S-structures' instead; he similarly refers to his revised version of deep structures as 'D-structures'. We shall follow this terminology to avoid confusion with the older model.

One such empty element is a TRACE: when an element is moved by a movement rule, it is suggested that it leaves a trace (symbolized by t) which is then available, in the S-structure, for semantic interpretation. This can be illustrated with *wh*-movement. We saw (p. 161) that the deep structure of *Which book did you buy?* might be (simplified):

> You bought which book

Let us now modify the previous analysis by indicating, first, in D-structure, the place to which the element may be moved (shown here with a dash), and second, in S-structure, the place from which it has been moved (with t):

> —— you bought which book? (D-structure)
> Which book did you buy t? (S-structure)

This is even more striking with:

> Which books do you think Bill says that Mary believes that John bought t?

In both sentences the presence of the trace not only indicates that *which books* has been moved, but also shows, for semantic interpretation, that the NP is (or was before movement) the object of *bought*. The trace is, it should be remembered, in S-structure, and so permits semantic interpretation from S-structure.

A similar analysis is possible for:

> *John seems to have won.*

The D-structure proposed for this is rather different from (and simpler than) the deep structure considered earlier:

> —— seems [s John to have won]

It is now very simple to derive the S-structure by moving *John* into the position indicated and leaving a trace:

> John seems t to have won

The trace shows that *John* is the subject of *to have won*. This is important because in a sentence such as *John is easy to please* the surface structure subject is the object of the subordinate verb in deep structure (p. 168). Let us consider the sentence:

> *John seems to have pleased.*

We must arrive at an S-structure with the trace in the correct position. We must not, therefore, have the following D-structure and S-structure (showing *John* as the object of *to please*):

> *—— seems to have pleased John
> *John seems to have pleased *t*

No less importantly, traces account for the facts with reflexives. We may compare:

> *John seems to have cut himself.*
> *John seems to have cut him.*

Normally the antecedent of a reflexive is in the same clause, but the antecedent of an ordinary pronoun is not (pp. 59, 164). Deep structure in the Standard Theory would have *John* in the embedded clause *John to have cut him(self)* and there would be no problem. The same facts can be accounted for in trace theory (provided that we again use co-indexing to show which NP is the antecedent of the reflexive). The D-structures of the sentences considered above would be:

> —— seems [$_S$ John$_1$ to have cut himself$_1$]
> —— seems [$_S$ John$_1$ to have cut him$_2$]

After movement we have the S-structures:

> John$_1$ seems [$_S$ t_1 to have cut
>   himself$_1$]
> John$_1$ seems [$_S$ t_1 to have cut him$_2$]

However, it will be seen that, in order to retain the observation that reflexives are co-referential with an NP in the same clause, we must, in the S-structure, co-index the trace with the NP that has been moved. In one case it will also be co-indexed with the pronoun (the reflexive); in the other it will not.

Slightly different arguments apply to the analysis of the passive. To begin with, because it has been shown that the semantic relation between active and passive sentences cannot be, or cannot always wholly be, accounted for by the transformation or by deep structure characteristics, active and passive sentences are no longer to be assigned nearly identical D-structures. Nevertheless, we can still show that the subject of the passive sentence is the object of the verb in D-structure if for *Dams are built by beavers*, for example, we have the D-structure:

—— are built dams by beavers

Movement of *dams* gives the S-structure:

Dams are built t by beavers

This, curiously, retains only half of the original insight about active and passive sentences. It shows that *dams* was the object of the verb in D-structure (as it would be in deep structure), but it does not suggest that *beavers* was the subject of the verb in D-structure. Yet there is some justification for this omission: it could be argued that with passivization objects 'become' subjects, but subjects do not become objects, and, in particular, that subjects (in deep structure) are absent altogether in agent-less passives. Because of this, there is a technical reason why trace theory can allow a trace to be left in object position but not in subject position – the fact that the subject position is already occupied. We should need an S-structure of the kind:

*Dams$_1$ t_2 are built t_1 by beavers$_2$

The subject position would be occupied by both *dams* and the trace of *beavers*; there is no problem about the trace in object position, because *beavers* has not moved there. But such technical arguments are far from convincing.

Traces are one type of empty element – the type that involves movement. But not all the rules that transformed deep structures into surface structures were movement rules. Equi-NP Deletion was not – it deleted elements instead of moving them. But the issues were very similar – elements that did not appear in surface structure had to be postulated for deep structure, to provide the correct semantic interpretation. For this second kind of relationship, a second type of empty element, symbolized by PRO, is proposed. Thus for the sentences

Bill wants to meet Mary.
I persuaded the doctor to examine John.

the suggested D-structures are

Bill$_1$ wants PRO$_1$ to meet Mary$_2$
I$_1$ persuaded the doctor$_2$ PRO$_2$ to examine John$_3$

Again it is necessary to indicate the co-indexing of NPs and PRO, to show that *Bill* is the subject of *to meet* and *the doctor* is the subject of *to examine*. Co-indexing also accounts for the facts concerning reflexives:

Bill$_1$ wants [$_S$ PRO$_1$ to help himself$_1$]
I$_1$ persuaded the doctor$_2$ [$_S$ PRO$_2$ to help himself$_2$]

Consideration of *t* and PRO and the contribution they make to the semantic interpretation crucially involves indexing to show co-referentiality. We have noted that there are some conditions concerning co-referentiality (pp. 59, 164), e.g. that a reflexive pronoun must normally be co-referential with (and so co-indexed with) an NP in the same clause, while an ordinary pronoun may not. But there is rather more to be said, and it is this subject that Chomsky refers to as BINDING. To say that an element is BOUND is to say that it is co-indexed and so co-referential with another; if it is not bound, it is FREE.

For the purposes of binding there are three kinds of NPs: ANAPHORS, pronominals and lexical NPs. Anaphors include not only all the reflexive pronouns such as *myself, yourself, herself*, etc., but also the reciprocals *each other* and *one another*. These are almost always co-referential with another NP in the same clause (*The boy hurt himself, John and Mary like each other*). Moreover, they cannot occur without an antecedent, since we cannot say *Himself came*; they must also agree in number and 'gender' (see p. 196) with their antecedents – *He washed himself/*herself*. Pronominals include, most importantly, the personal pronouns *I/me, he/him, you*, etc. They may refer to an NP already mentioned or to someone or something that is derivable from the context. But they may not refer to an NP within the same clause. We cannot say **I hurt me* while *He hurt him* cannot mean that he hurt himself. Finally, there are lexical NPs which do not normally take their references from any other NPs, e.g. *the boy, John*. There are some exceptions to this; certain expressions such as *the idiot, the bastard* are used as if they were pronominals, e.g.:

John started talking and the idiot gave away the whole secret.

This is also true, especially in journalism, of expressions like *the president*, which may refer to an already mentioned *Mr Reagan*, or *the speedy striker* which may refer to a previously named footballer.

We have so far assumed that the issues of co-referentiality relate essentially to elements within the same clause, but Chomsky points out that the rules apply within NPs as well as Ss, for we may equally quote:

> *John's picture of himself*   (*John hurt himself.*)
> *John's picture of him*   (*John hurt him.*)

Just as the rules concerning co-referentiality apply only within the clause, the minimal S, and not within the larger S which may contain other Ss, so too they apply only within the minimal NP. We may compare:

> [$_S$ John said [$_S$ that Henry hurt himself]]
> [$_{NP}$ John's [$_{NP}$ son's picture of himself]]

Himself in the first can only be co-referential with *Henry*, in the same clause, and not with *John*; in the second, for similar reasons, it can only be referential with *son*, which is in the same minimal NP, and not with *John*.

Traditional grammar provides no name for minimal NPs, as it provides 'clause' for minimal Ss, but Chomsky subsumes both under GOVERNING CATEGORY (for which he provides a technical definition). He then further suggests that:

> an anaphor must be bound in its governing category;
> a pronominal must be free in its governing category;
> a lexical NP must be free everywhere.

What this says is that an anaphor (a reflexive pronoun or reciprocal) is always co-referential with another NP within the minimal S (the clause) or the minimal NP, that other types of pronoun will not be co-referential within these minimal categories (but they will often be co-referential with NPs outside them) and that lexical NPs are not co-referential with other NPs. It is not, however, sufficient merely to know that an NP is bound – co-referential and co-indexed; we also need to state, especially in the case of the empty NPs, PRO and trace, what are the NPs with which they are co-referential.

There is no difficulty about traces. They are always co-indexed with the NPs that have been moved and are also subject to the usual binding conditions. This is clear in the examples we discussed:

John$_1$ seems [$_S$ t_1 to have cut himself]
John$_1$ seems [$_S$ t_1 to have cut him]

The trace is co-referential with *John*. The anaphor *himself* is co-referential with the trace, but the pronominal *him* is not. *Himself*, therefore, but not *him*, is co-referential with *John*.

The co-referentiality of PRO cannot be predicted so easily. We may compare:

John persuaded the boy to leave.
John promised the boy to leave.

In both of these sentences PRO will be the subject of *to leave*, but it will be co-indexed with the object of the main clause *the boy* in the first, and the subject of the main clause *John* in the second, since with PERSUADE it is the boy who should leave, but with PROMISE it is John who should leave:

John$_1$ persuaded the boy$_2$ PRO$_2$ to leave
John$_1$ promised the boy$_2$ PRO$_1$ to leave

With a verb such as WANT co-indexing will be with the subject:

John$_1$ wanted PRO$_1$ to leave

With other predicates it may be that PRO is not co-indexed at all:

It is not clear what to do.
(It is not clear what PRO to do)

for the subject of *do* is unstated. Similarly with *John is easy to please*, we need an unindexed PRO as the subject of *to please* (see p. 168 where it is indicated by Δ).

The co-referentiality of PRO depends, then, on the lexical items, PERSUADE, PROMISE, WANT, etc. This involves yet another issue known as CONTROL. It is suggested that we must distinguish three kinds of predicate (the embedded Ss): those that have a subject controlled PRO (PROMISE, WANT, etc.); those that have a non-subject controlled PRO (PERSUADE, ORDER, etc.); and those that have uncontrolled PROs (CLEAR, EASY, etc.). The verbs and adjectives that are associated with these types of control must, of course, be specified in the lexicon.

Much of the generative machinery of the early models is absent from this more recent model. There is far more concentration on conditions, constraints and filters. Surprisingly, perhaps, Chomsky has suggested that there is only one movement rule which he terms 'alpha movement' and which says 'Move any category anywhere'. There are, however, sufficient strict conditions to ensure that the only categories that can be moved and the only places to which they can be moved are very limited indeed (mostly those of NP movement and *wh*-movement that we have discussed). But the technicalities are too complex for this volume.

5.6 *Some theoretical issues*

In the discussions and proposals concerning TG a number of general theoretical issues have arisen. Four will be discussed here.

(1) In *Syntactic Structures* a distinction was made between 'discovery procedures' and 'evaluation procedures'. The structuralists had been largely concerned with discovering the phonemes, the morphemes and the ICs, whereas Chomsky argued that we should, as linguists, be more concerned with evaluating grammars, i.e. models of description. But there is no real conflict between discovery and evaluation. We must both construct theoretical models and attempt to state the facts within such models. It is to some degree true that the structuralists thought that there were no great theoretical issues to be solved. They believed that language had a structure, rather as a body has a skeleton, and that it was their duty to discover it. But Chomsky's point was essentially that the 'structure' of language, if that term may be used, is far more abstract and cannot simply be discovered; we need rather to discuss how we are to deal with the problem of language, to evaluate rather than simply to discover. Yet it was not wholly true that the structuralists took no interest in evaluation. Hockett's 'Two models of grammatical description' (see p. 106) was essentially concerned with evaluating alternative models. Nevertheless, Chomsky's arguments were, quite rightly, influential in making linguists aware of the need to consider and evaluate the models they were using.

(2) In *Aspects of the Theory of Syntax* Chomsky introduced the notions of COMPETENCE and PERFORMANCE (though these are, in most essential respects, the same as de Saussure's *langue* ('language') and *parole* ('speaking')). Competence he defined as the ideal speaker-hearer's knowledge of his language, whereas performance is the actual use of the language. This will account for the fact that language has numerous false starts, deviation from rules, changes of plan in mid-course and so on. (We noted an example of this on p. 67.) Now it is perfectly true that, in practice, we must idealize. We must set up a coherent, consistent description of a language, even if an inspection of the use of language shows inconsistency and incoherence. This is probably true of all sciences. But idealization is, to some extent, a purely practical matter and it does not follow that there is a clear theoretical distinction between competence and performance.

To begin with, there is a problem with the idea of the speaker-hearer's knowledge of his language. Although Chomsky suggested that we make use of our intuitions in arriving at the linguistic description, he has argued that this knowledge may be unconscious, that we may be unaware of it. But what is 'unconscious' knowledge? A familiar philosophical distinction is between 'knowing-how' and 'knowing-that'. We may know how to swim or how to ride a bicycle without having any knowledge (i.e. of the knowing-that kind) what it is that we do. If knowledge of our language is merely knowing-how, there is no issue; all linguists would agree that we know how to speak and to interpret what we hear. But Chomsky wants more than this – his grammar is essentially a description of the speaker-hearer's knowledge. He has even suggested that we may say, if 'knowing' is misleading, that the speaker 'cognizes'. But using different terms will not help. Unless the speaker knows his language in some kind of knowing-that sense, it is difficult to see how the linguist can describe that knowledge, except in terms of the neurological functions of the brain. But neurology is not the same as grammar or linguistics.

One good point that has come out of the discussion is that we must recognize that speakers are creative: they may produce new sentences all the time, sentences that have never been uttered or written before. The structuralists were strongly inclined to concentrate on 'texts', on what had actually been said or written, whereas generative linguists are more concerned with what is possible in language, and this is surely correct. Nevertheless, we still need, very largely, to look at texts, at actual real language in order to predict what is or is not possible. We may, of course, also use our own judgements about what is or is not an English sentence. But there are dangers here; it is all too easy to invent examples to prove a point, to exclude others, and even to make judgements about grammaticality that suit the theory. It has sometimes been said of asterisked forms in theoretical works that they are merely those English sentences that would contradict the proposals being made.

(3) In his views on competence and performance Chomsky came down on the side of the mentalists, in the mentalist/mechanist controversy. Bloomfield was a self-proclaimed mechanist, claiming that all linguistic phenomena could be explained in terms of physical events in the context and in the brains of the individuals concerned. The mentalists, whom he condemned, spoke about the 'mind' and mental events and processes. More recently, Chomsky has suggested that languages have a highly restricted set of principles that are innate in us, and that it is the task of the linguists to establish what these principles are. The child does not learn these principles any more than he 'learns how to breathe or ... to have two arms'. Only this fact can explain how it is that a child can learn a language so quickly. Languages are different, but given that the child already has these basic principles, he can develop a strategy for deciding what are the rules of the language to which he is exposed. But it is difficult to see how this can be proved. Certainly, human beings have an innate, intuitive ability to learn and to speak languages that other creatures do not. (Experiments with chimpanzees and gorillas have demonstrated the intelligence of these higher apes, but not an ability to learn much language.) But humans have the ability for other quite remarkable intellectual achievements – in music and mathematics, for example, and these can hardly be innate, for they are, in genetic terms, very recent acquisitions. Moreover, it is by no means clear what kind of principles there might be; many of the proposals made in even the most recent generative grammars often fail to work for languages other than English.

(4) Chomsky also claims that there are universal characteristics of language and that these, too, should be the concern of the linguist. Of course, if the linguistic principles are innate, they must also be universal (at least, if we take into account the established fact that any child from any racial group can learn

any language). But there is no very strong evidence for the universal principles; they are largely inferred from the assumption of innateness and not proved by empirical investigation. It may be that all languages have nouns and verbs. They may all have subjects and objects, though that is very doubtful (see pp. 75–7). Even if we find features shared by all languages, we cannot conclude that they are universal, in the sense of being necessary characteristics of all languages. They may be shared because of a common linguistic ancestor or because of language contact and borrowing.

Most of these issues are matters of speculation and unlikely to be resolved in the near future. Moreover, they are not wholly relevant to linguistic theory and practice. It is perfectly possible to be a follower of TG and still reject mentalism, innateness or universals, or, alternatively, to be a structuralist and accept them.

Appendix. Grammatical Categories in English

A. *Gender*

1. English has no gender: the nouns of English cannot be classified in terms of agreement with articles, adjectives (or verbs).

2.1 There are in English pairs of words of the type of *stallion/mare*, *ram/ewe*, *boar/sow*, *uncle/aunt*, *brother/sister*. But this is a lexical feature, not a grammatical one – related to sex, not gender. We ought to talk of these, then, in terms of 'male' and 'female' not 'masculine' and 'feminine'.

2.2 English has a suffix *-ess* used in, for example, *authoress*, *princess*, *duchess*. But this too is a lexical feature. It is not regular since we have no *teacheress*, *doctoress*, *kingess*, etc., and it is not even regular morphologically. This is a matter of derivation, but not of grammatical gender.

2.3 Within the same lexical area we have names for small creatures – *foal*, *lamb*, *piglet*. There is often a quartet – the generic name, the name of the male, the name of the female and the name of the young (*sheep*, *ram*, *ewe*, *lamb*), though there are fewer distinctions in some cases (*dog* is generic and male, *cow* usually generic and female, *foal* and *colt* distinguish two kinds of young horse, and there is also *filly*). Note that here too there is a very irregular kind of derivation, *piglet*, *duckling*, *gosling*.

3.1 The choice of the pronouns is almost entirely a matter of sex – *he* refers to male, *she* to female and *it* to sexless objects or optionally to animals even when their sex is known. If we divide up the words in English according to the pronouns used we find not three classes but seven since some words are referred to by two or three of the pronouns:

he	man, boy, uncle
she	woman, girl, aunt
it	table, chair, tree
he, she	doctor, teacher, cousin
he, it	bull, ram, boar
she, it	ewe, sow, ship
he, she, it	cat, dog, thrush

There is one odd man out here – *ship*, and we could have added *car*, *boat*, *engine*. It could be argued that since these are sometimes referred to as 'she' that English has gender, since this is not a matter of sex but of the arbitrary kind of classification found in French *la porte*, etc. But, first, these are very few in number (and we should not wish to build a grammatical category on a few examples) and they belong to a clearly defined class of mechanical things. We can add to this class, and in recent years *plane* and *hovercraft* have been added. This is not then a matter of grammatical gender at all but simply that *she* is used for females and mechanical objects (a class defined semantically).

Where there is co-reference with reflexives (pp. 59, 164, 189), it might seem we have agreement within the clause, and a similar point could be made with emphatic forms with -*self* since we find *The boy himself . . .* and *The boy hurt himself* not **The boy herself . . .* or **The boy hurt herself*. But this is still determined by sex, not grammatical gender. The choice of one of the following will depend on a judgement about sex:

> *The dog bit himself.*
> *The dog bit herself.*
> *The dog bit itself.*

B. Number

1. English clearly has number in *cat/cats*, *man/men*, etc., and the concord restrictions (a) with verbs *The man comes*, *The men come* and (b) with demonstratives *this man*, *these men*.
2. One slight anomaly is that the present tense forms of the verb are not simply divided morphologically into singular and plural. The division is rather between the 'third person singular' and the rest – *He comes* vs. *I come*, *they come*. The only forms which divide simply into two morphological groups are those of the past tense of BE – *was* and *were*, *I was*, *they were* (*you* presumably can be regarded as a plural form even when it refers to a single person).
3. Morphologically the spoken and the written forms of the noun differ with regard to number classification (see p. 31).
4.1 Number in English is closely associated with a category that the traditional grammar books have largely missed – that of 'countable'/'unaccountable' nouns (sometimes called 'count'/'mass'). The distinction is between words such as *cat*, *book*, *road* on the one hand, and *butter*, *petrol*, *bread* on the other. The chief differences grammatically are that the uncountables generally have no plural forms (*butters, *petrols, *breads) and that they do not occur with

the indefinite article *a* or *an* (**a butter*, **a petrol*, **a bread*). The contrast is in fact seen clearly in *bread* and *loaf*. The unfortunate foreigner who does not know that *bread* is an uncountable is liable to say 'Can I have a bread?' or 'There were two breads on the table'. In both cases, of course, he could have used *loaf* and been grammatical. It is not, however, only the indefinite article that is involved in the countable/uncountable distinction. In addition there is the possibility of no article at all and also of the 'weak' form of 'some' (phonetically [səm]). Countables do not occur (in the singular) without an article, though uncountables do – *Butter is . . .*, but not **Cat is . . .* Uncountables alone occur with the weak form of 'some', *Would you like some bread?*, but not **Would you like some cat?* (Notice, however, that there is a strong form [sʌm] which does occur with countables – *Some cat has stolen the fish*, or Winston Churchill's famous *Some chicken, some neck*.) We can illustrate the distinction of uncountable and countable in a table (using ø – zero – to mean 'having no article'):

	a	some ([səm])	ø
cat	√	—	—
butter	—	√	√

4.2 It is, however, possible to 'switch' countables into uncountables and vice versa. We could say *Would you like some giraffe?* to people who eat giraffe, or *A petrol I like very much is Brand X*. Countable nouns, that is to say, may be treated as uncountables if they are regarded as food and uncountable as countable when the meaning is 'a kind of . . .' But the semantics alone is not enough, as shown by *bread/loaf*, or by the fact that we cannot say *a soap* meaning 'a cake of soap'; it is a purely linguistic fact that *bread* and *soap* are uncountable and *loaf* countable. Some words belong to both classes, e.g., *cake*: *Would you like a cake? Would you like some cake?* (where *loaf* and *bread* are, respectively, the corresponding forms).

5. Some singular nouns ('collectives') are commonly used with plural verbs – *The committee have decided*, *England have won the World Cup*. Note, however, that while the verb is plural the demonstratives cannot be. We cannot say **These committee have decided*.

6. Some nouns have no singular – *scissors*, *trousers*, *pliers*, etc. All are semantically 'pairs'. These raise an interesting point with the numerals. It might be thought that numerals above *one* can all be used with plural nouns (*three cats*, *seventy dogs*, etc.). But these plural forms cannot be used with any numerals since we have no **one scissors* or **ten scissors*, etc. But they can be used with the plural forms of the demonstratives – *these scissors*.

7. There are some anomalous plural forms, especially *police* and *clergy*. These are unlikely with numerals – **thirty police* would usually be rejected in favour of *thirty policemen* – and also unlikely with plural demonstratives, **these police*. They are then rather like the form

committee used with plural verbs ('collectives'). Note, however, that *people* is in all respects plural (*these people, thirty people*, etc.), and so, too, probably is *cattle*.

8. A minor anomaly is provided by *a dozen* which functions just like *twelve – a dozen eggs* (note that *a score, a gross,* do not function in this way). Similarly, *a lot of* functions like *many – a lot of men are* . . ., and *kind of*, rather like *such – these kind of people* (though this may be thought sub-standard).

C. Tense

1. Morphologically English has two tenses only, as exemplified by *He likes/He liked, He takes/He took*. These are most plausibly referred to as 'present' and 'past'. Other verbal categories, the perfect, the progressive, etc., are achieved by the use of the auxiliaries BE and HAVE.

2. There is, then, a real sense in which English has no future tense. There are ways of referring to future time, but this is no more a justification for a future tense than the fact that we have ways of referring to near and far (*here/there*) is evidence of a 'spatial' tense.

2.1 The paradigm *I shall, thou wilt (you will), he will*, then *we shall, you will, they will* is purely a grammarian's invention. *I will, we will* and especially the contracted *I'll, we'll* are as much part of the pattern as *I shall, we shall*. Careful investigation has shown that there is no evidence that *I shall, we shall* are the forms regularly used.

2.2 *Shall* and *will* are modal auxiliaries functioning exactly as *can* and *may*. If we establish them as markers of an English tense we ought equally to recognize tenses for the other modals.

2.3 *Will* is used for functions other than future time reference:

> *I'll come, if you ask me.* (willingness)
> *She'll sit for hours.* (habit)
> *That'll be John.* (probability)
> *Oil will float on water.* (general truth)

Note in particular the syntactic contrast of *will* for future and *will* for willingness in:

> *John will come tomorrow.* (futurity)
> *If John comes* . . .
> *John will come tomorrow.* (willingness)
> *If John will come* . . .

Will then has futurity as only one of several meanings. Similarly, *shall* is used also for threat or promise: *You shall have it tomorrow.*

2.4 There are other ways of referring to future time:

The progressive	*I'm flying to Paris tomorrow.*
going to	*I'm going to ask you a question.*
The simple present	*Term starts on Monday.*
about to	*He's about to speak.*

Going to is particularly important. It differs phonetically from the progressive form of *go*. Contrast:

I'm going to London.
I'm going to talk.

The latter but not the former can be [gənə].

2.5 All these points militate against the traditional view of *will* and *shall* as makers of the future. Why these? Why any future. If meaning is the test, then, it has been suggested, nouns have tense – *ex-wife* is past, *fiancée* future and *grandfather* pluperfect!

3. English past tense does not refer only to past time. It has two other functions.

3.1 Clearly the past tense is used for past time reference in e.g.

He came yesterday.

Notice, however, that we have also a past progressive (i.e. forms that are past *and* progressive),

He was coming yesterday,

a past perfect,

He had come the day before,

and even a past perfect progressive

He had been coming the day before.

But *came, was, had* mark these all as past (with past time reference).

3.2 The past tense is also used in reported speech in accordance with a 'sequence of tenses' rule:

He said he went to London every day
(his words were 'I go to London every day').
The use of *went* here is determined solely by the use of the past tense form *said*; it does not itself indicate past time, and in many languages a past tense form would not be used. Notice, however, that we can use a present tense form if the speaker wishes to indicate that the reported statement is still true:

The ancient Greeks discovered that the world is
round, but the Romans maintained that it was flat.

(We could replace *is* by *was* here, but we cannot replace *was* by *is* without implying that the world is flat.)

3.3 The past tense is often used only to indicate 'tentativeness', improbability or impossibility. There are, perhaps, three separate uses of this kind. First, in statements and questions it is more tentative or even more polite:

I wanted to ask you something.
Could you pass me the salt?

Secondly, it is used with 'impossible' wishes:

I wish I knew.
I wish I had one.

Thirdly, it is used for unreal conditions. Compare:

If John comes, I shall leave.
If John came, I should leave.

The verbs in the second sentence are past tense; the difference in meaning is that in the second there is an assumption that the condition will not be fulfilled – it is 'unreal'. There is no point, then, in talking of 'conditional' forms of the verb; English has no special conditional forms, but uses tense to distinguish real and unreal conditions.

3.4 From this it also follows that English has no subjunctive. What is sometimes referred to as the subjunctive is in fact merely the past tense form in impossible wishes or in unreal conditions (*I wish I knew, If John came...*). One form that might seem to belie this in that it seems to differ from the past tense form in *were* is *If I were ...* as compared with *I was there yesterday*. But the remarkable thing here is that it is not *were* that is exceptional but *was*. The paradigm of *I/you/he/we/they were* is wholly regular, since with all other verbs there is only one past tense form – *I/you/he/we/they loved*. *Was* then is the odd man out, a special form used with singular pronouns and nouns when tense is used for past time reference. Clearly then there is no evidence of a special 'subjunctive' form. The other form sometimes referred to as the subjunctive is in fact the uninflected 'simple' form:

God save the Queen.
If that be so ...

But this is the same as the 'infinitive', the 'imperative' and the present tense form without *-s* (except for BE). Here English comes closest to being an isolating language (p. 52) in its verbal system, and subjunctive is essentially a category belonging to highly inflected languages!

Sources and References

p. 11. Definition of grammar: Chomsky, N., *Current Issues in Linguistic Theory* (The Hague: Mouton, 1964), p. 9.

p. 20. Tigrinya: all examples from modern Ethiopian languages are from the author's own research.

p. 23. Japanese: Kuno, S., *The Structure of the Japanese Language* (Cambridge, Mass., and London: MIT Press, 1973).

p. 47. Bloomfield, L., *Language* (New York: Holt, and London: Allen & Unwin, 1935), p. 178.

p. 52. von Humboldt, W., *Über die Verschiedenheit des menslichen Sprachbaues* (Berlin, 1836; Facsimile reprint, 1960), pp. 135ff.

p. 55. Dionysius Thrax: Robins, R. H., *A Short History of Linguistics* (London: Longman, 1967), pp. 33–4.

p. 57. Fries, C. C., *The Structure of English* (New York: Harcourt Brace Jovanovich, 1952, and London: Longmans, Green & Co., 1957).

p. 63. Hockett, C. F., *A Course in Modern Linguistics* (New York: Macmillan, 1958), pp. 226–7.

p. 68. Bloomfield, L., *Language*, p. 170.

p. 73. Nesfield, J. C., *Manual of English Grammar and Composition* (1898 and thereafter), pp. 5, 101.

p. 76. Lisu: Li, C. N., and Thomson, S. A., 'Subject and topic: a new typology', in Li, C. N. (ed.), *Subject and Topic* (New York: Academic Press, 1976), pp. 458–89.
Dyirbal: Dixon, R. W. M., 'Ergativity', in *Language*, 55 (1977), pp. 59–138 (see especially p. 61).

p. 81. Algonquian: Bloomfield, L., *Language*, p. 272.

p. 88. Malagasy: Keenan, E. L., 'Remarkable subjects in Malagasy', in Li, C. N. (ed.), *Subject and Topic*, pp. 247–301.

p. 97. Menomini: Hockett, C. F., *A Course in Modern Linguistics*, p. 217.

p. 99ff. Bloomfield, L., *Language*, Chs. 10 and 13.

p. 103. Hockett, C. F., 'Problems of morphemic analysis', in *Language*, 23 (1947), pp. 321–43. Reprinted in Joos, M. (ed.), *Readings in Linguistics* (New York: American Council of Learned Societies, 1958), pp. 229–42.

p. 106. Hockett, C. F., 'Two models of grammatical description', in *Word*, 10 (1954), pp. 210–31. Reprinted in Joos, M. (ed.), *Readings in Linguistics*, pp. 386–99.

p. 108. A number of examples in this section are from Matthews, P. H., *Morphology* (Cambridge: Cambridge University Press, 1976).

p. 113. Hockett: 'Problems of morphemic analysis', see ref. to p. 103.

p. 114. Oromo: Moreno, M. M., *Grammatica della lingua Galla* (Milano: Montadori, 1939).

p. 118. Italian: Hall, R. A., Jr., *Introductory Linguistics* (Philadelphia and New York: Chilton Books, 1964), pp. 141–2.

p. 119. Chomsky, N., and Halle, M., *The Sound Pattern of English* (New York: Harper and Row, 1968), pp. 52–4.

p. 121. IC analysis: Wells, R. S., 'Immediate constituents', in *Language*, 23 (1947), pp. 81–111. Reprinted in Joos, M. (ed.), *Readings in Linguistics*, pp. 186–207.

p. 133. Palmer, H. E., and Blandford, F. G., *A Grammar of Spoken English*, 2nd ed. (Cambridge: Heffer, 1939), pp. 124–5.

p. 149. Chomsky, N., *Syntactic Structures* (The Hague: Mouton, 1957); *The Logical Structure of Linguistic Theory* (New York: Plenum, 1975); *Aspects of the Theory of Syntax* (Cambridge, Mass.: MIT Press, 1965); *Lectures on Government and Binding* (Dordrecht: Foris, 1982). Chomsky has written many other books and articles; quite the best modern account is Radford, A., *Transformational Syntax: A Student's Guide to Chomsky's Extended Standard Theory* (Cambridge: Cambridge University Press, 1981).

p. 172. Constraints: the original work is Ross, J. R., *Constraints on Variables in Syntax* (Indiana University Linguistics Club, 1968).

p. 180. Fillmore, C. J., 'The case for case', in Bach, E., and Harms, R. T. (eds.), *Universals in Linguistic Theory* (New York: Rinehart and Winston, 1968), pp. 1–68.

p. 182. Generative semantics: see e.g. Seuren, P. A. (ed.), *Semantic Syntax* (London: Oxford University Press, 1974).

p. 192. de Saussure, F., *Cours de linguistique générale* (Payot: Paris, 1916); translated as *Course in General Linguistics* by Baskin, W. (New York: McGraw-Hill, 1959), pp. 23–32, 7–15.

p. 193. Chomsky: *Language and Mind*, enlarged ed. (New York: Harcourt Brace Jovanovich, 1972), p. 171.

Further Reading

Some of the general topics in Chapter 1 are further discussed in Hall, R. A., Jr., *Linguistics and Your Language* (New York: Doubleday, 1960).

For American structuralism the most readable is C. F. Hockett's *A Course in Modern Linguistics* (New York: Macmillan, 1958), while a good basic book on linguistics is Robins, R. H., *General Linguistics: An Introductory Survey* (London: Longman, 3rd ed., 1980).

Apart from *Syntactic Structures* most of Chomsky's publications are very difficult for the non-specialist. An excellent, but not easy, account of the present position is A. Radford's *Transformational Syntax: A Student's Guide to Chomsky's Extended Standard Theory* (Cambridge: Cambridge University Press, 1981).

For English there is Quirk, R., and Greenbaum, S., *A University Grammar of English* (London: Longman, 1973); and Palmer, F. R., *The English Verb* (London: Longman, 1974).

Index

(This index refers only to pages on which the more important topics are explained or discussed in detail)

Indicative, *see* Mood
Indirect object, 71, 76
Infinitive, 50
Inflection, 64–5
Intensifier, 56
Internal clause filter, 179
Intonation, 29–31
Intransitive, 71
Island constraint, 173–4
Isolating, 52

Juncture, 46

Kernel sentences, 155

Labelled bracketing, 127
Latin, 16–19, 20, 21, 76, 77
Lexicon, 133–8
Liaison, 116–18
'Logic', 21–3

Masculine, *see* Gender
Meaning (*see also* Form), 40
Mentalism, 193
Mood, 78, 86–7
Morph, *see* Allomorph
Morpheme, 99–106
Morphology, 13, 31–2, 34–5, 77, 78,
   81–2, 95, 97–8, 196–8
Morphophonemics, 106, 156, 157
Morphosyntactic, 54, 64
Movement, 150, 160, 164–5, 174–8,
   185–7, 191

Neuter, *see* Gender
Normative, 15–27
Noun, 38–9, 58
Number, 23, 31–3, 34–5, 77, 78,
   81–2, 95, 97–8, 196–8

Object, 71, 74, 75–6

Paradigm, 71, 74, 75–6
Parsing, 73–4
Parts of speech, 38–9, 55–65, 134
Passive (*see also* Voice)
Performance, 192
Person, 78, 82–5
Phoneme, 100–101
Phonology, 45–6, 100
Phrase, 70–71, 73
Phrase structure grammar, 127–33

Plural, *see* Number
Predicate, 66
Preposition, 59, 64
Pro-forms, 59, 68
Pronoun, 37–8, 58–9, 195–6

Quantifier, 183
Questions, 20, 164

Raising, 168–71
Recursion, 141–4, 161
Reflexive, 73
Regular, 110, 111
Rules, 15–27

Sandhi, 108, 116
Selectional restrictions, 137–8, 153–4
Semantics (*see also* Meaning),
Sentence, 66–77, 121–48
Setential subject constraint, 176
Singular, *see* Number
Speech (and Writing), 27–34, 42–3
Standard language, 25–6
Stress, 45–6, 64
Structuralism, 121
Subcategorization, 134–7
Subjacency condition, 176
Subject, 71, 74, 75–6, 93
Subjunctive, *see* Mood
Subordination, 59, 72, 73, 143
Superlative, 63, 65
Surface structure, 157, 159, 161,
   184–5
Syntax, 13, 48, 53, 99, 121

Tense, 38, 77, 78, 85–6, 87, 198–200
Trace, 185–7, 190
Transformation, 150–55
Transformational generative
   grammar, 149–94
Transitive, 71

Verb, 58, 62
Voice, 78, 88–9
Vowel harmony, 45

Wh-words, 160–61, 164–5
Word, 41–9
Word classes, 55–65, 134
Writing, *see* Speech

'X-bar syntax', 139–41

FOR THE BEST IN PAPERBACKS, LOOK FOR THE

In every corner of the world, on every subject under the sun, Penguin represents quality and variety – the very best in publishing today.

For complete information about books available from Penguin – including Puffins, Penguin Classics and Arkana – and how to order them, write to us at the appropriate address below. Please note that for copyright reasons the selection of books varies from country to country.

In the United Kingdom: Please write to *Dept E.P., Penguin Books Ltd, Harmondsworth, Middlesex, UB7 0DA.*

If you have any difficulty in obtaining a title, please send your order with the correct money, plus ten per cent for postage and packaging, to *PO Box No 11, West Drayton, Middlesex*

In the United States: Please write to *Dept BA, Penguin, 299 Murray Hill Parkway, East Rutherford, New Jersey 07073*

In Canada: Please write to *Penguin Books Canada Ltd, 2801 John Street, Markham, Ontario L3R 1B4*

In Australia: Please write to the *Marketing Department, Penguin Books Australia Ltd, P.O. Box 257, Ringwood, Victoria 3134*

In New Zealand: Please write to the *Marketing Department, Penguin Books (NZ) Ltd, Private Bag, Takapuna, Auckland 9*

In India: Please write to *Penguin Overseas Ltd, 706 Eros Apartments, 56 Nehru Place, New Delhi, 110019*

In the Netherlands: Please write to *Penguin Books Nederland B.V., Postbus 195, NL–1380AD Weesp*

In West Germany: Please write to *Penguin Books Ltd, Friedrichstrasse 10–12, D–6000 Frankfurt/Main 1*

In Spain: Please write to *Longman Penguin España, Calle San Nicolas 15, E–28013 Madrid*

In Italy: Please write to *Penguin Italia s.r.l., Via Como 4, I-20096 Pioltello (Milano)*

In France: Please write to *Penguin Books Ltd, 39 Rue de Montmorency, F-75003 Paris*

In Japan: Please write to *Longman Penguin Japan Co Ltd, Yamaguchi Building, 2-12-9 Kanda Jimbocho, Chiyoda-Ku, Tokyo 101*